# Family

# the Forming Center

# Family the Forming Center

Revised and Expanded

## Marjorie J. Thompson

UPPER
ROOM BOOKS®
NASHVILLE

FAMILY THE FORMING CENTER
A Vision of the Role of Family in Spiritual Formation
© 1996 by Marjorie J. Thompson
All rights reserved.

The Upper Room web site: www.upperroom.org

The excerpt from a poem by Mary Hynes-Berry in chapter 4 is used by permission of the poet.

Page 159 serves as an extension of this copyright page.

Art Direction: Michele Wetherbee
Design: Laura Beers
Fifth printing: 2004

LIBRARY OF CONGRESS CATALOGING-IN-PUBLICATION
Thompson, Marjorie J., 1953–
        Family the forming center : a vision of the role of family in spiritual formation / Marjorie J. Thompson.—Rev. and expanded.
        p.    cm.
        Includes bibliographical references.
        ISBN: 0-8358-0798-3
        1. Family—Religious life. 2. Family—Religious aspects—Christianity. 3. Christian education of children. 4. Spiritual formation. I. Title.
BV4526.2. T47 1996                              96-32881
248.4—dc20                                            CIP

In gratitude to my mother,

Jean Thompson Seely,

whose love and faith have formed
my spirit in countless ways
and to my father,

W. J. Sinclair

Thompson,

whose memory has profoundly
shaped my commitment to the church.

# Contents

~

# Acknowledgments

~

THE ORIGINAL VERSION OF THIS BOOK was published in response to a consultation on family spirituality sponsored by The Upper Room more than a decade ago. The consultation was both timely and ahead of its time. Significantly, the level of interest in the role of families has risen dramatically since then—both in church and culture. While politicians and sociologists debate issues of "family values," major denominations have begun to attend more seriously to the significance of this basic unit of social cohesion, not only for moral character development but for spiritual formation.

The expanded materials in this edition have evolved over several years of working with parents, grandparents, educators, and pastors in workshops and conferences on the subject of family spirituality. I owe a debt of gratitude to each participant in these events. Their stories and insights have enriched, stretched, and reshaped my own perspectives and have contributed significantly to the added content of this book.

Those whose vision and wisdom contributed to the first edition remain indelibly connected to my work on family spirituality. It was the invitation and encouragement of Janice Grana and Charla Honea that enticed me to write my first book. The editing and research skills of Jill Reddig, Glenda Webb, and Sarah Linn shepherded me through the process. Dolores Leckey, Wendy Wright, Gwen White, Judy Smith, Willie Teague, and Mary Ruth Coffman all offered important insights, resources, and personal stories to draw on. I am deeply indebted to each one and bless God for their many faith-filled gifts. Of course, for a married person (like myself), no book can be written without the support and sacrifice of one's spouse. I remain profoundly grateful to my husband, John, for taking many precious evening hours to review and critique the original manuscript.

This new edition owes its life to the attentive eye of acquisitions editor JoAnn Miller and to the dedicated labors of associate editor Rita Collett. I am deeply thankful to each for the foresight, encouragement, and perseverance that gently but firmly prodded me through revisions at a time I felt I could not possibly manage another task.

My intent in this book is to make a meaningful contribution to pastors, educators, lay leaders, and interested families within the church. If the thesis raises questions, it is my fond hope that such questions will lead to lively and fruitful dialogue within the church, to the glory of the One whose name we bear.

# Introduction

~

WE LIVE IN AN AGE OF HIGH technology, high-speed living, and high anxiety. Exponentially rapid change has characterized this second half of the twentieth century, and the consequent social dislocations have resulted in enormous stress. It seems to me no accident that people of faith have begun to search with new intensity for a spiritual center. Surely the explosion of interest in spirituality among members of many churches and among many who are disaffected or disaffiliated from churches is evidence of our crying need for depth and focus. We long for the stability and continuity of eternal truths amid the rapidly shifting sands of cultural values and patterns.

The pace and complexity of our modern world have impacted families with particularly destructive force. Cultural stresses and loss of normative values have been disproportionately borne by the essential unit of our society, leaving the family in dire need of support and healing. If we are going to look to spirituality for a sense of direction as individuals and church communities, we must look to it also as a primary resource for families, which constitute a mediating structure between the individual and the larger church.

For better or worse, family life is inevitably formative in a spiritual as well as a physical and emotional sense. The intent of this book is to suggest that families of committed faith are the initial and most natural context for the positive spiritual formation of children. My approach will be twofold: to show how the family is intrinsically formative spiritually and to indicate how various spiritual practices may realistically support the health and growth of the family within its larger communities.

I have no intention of pitting family against church in my thesis. I want, rather, to acknowledge the enormous impact families have on the psychodynamic development of individuals, especially children, and to affirm that this formative power has an intrinsic relationship to spiritual development. The church provides the larger framework of spiritual teaching and tradition within which families of faith find and keep their center. The guidance of the church supports such families in developing healthy, reconciling relationships within the home.

Perhaps it is best to point out from the start that whether a family's impact is constructive or destructive, it is not ultimate. In cases where families have offered no model for faith or where the model has proved distorted, narrow, or superficial, individuals often have showed remarkable courage and resiliency in overcoming their negative inheritance. The capacity to transcend one's background depends on a number of factors, including personal strength of character, independence, and inner freedom; the mitigating influence of peers, teachers, and healthy communities of faith; and often professional therapeutic help. There are limits, of course, to our ability to transcend personal history. Sometimes we think we are freer than we really are; for example, conscious choices to avoid our parents' errors are often subverted by unconscious forces so that we become more like our parents than we might wish to be. Still, I believe that neither a particular family nor a particular congregation can ultimately determine a person's faith. Only God, whose spirit is free to create and recreate, has ultimate power to shape us.

When I speak of spiritual formation in a general sense, I am also speaking of families broadly; but when dealing specifically with Christian spiritual formation—my basic concern—I am then speaking specifically of families within the church. I do not object to the designation "Christian family" when referring to families comprised of baptized members of the church, although I frequently use alternative phrases, such as "families of faith."[1]

It is within the framework of these considerations that my thesis on the primacy of the family in spiritual nurture needs to be understood.

To propose that ordinary lay families within the church play a central role in personal spiritual formation may strike some readers as unusual. An all-too-common misperception in the church is that *real* spirituality is the purview of monks, ministers, and missionaries. Culturally, we are in the habit of separating the sacred from the secular—an indication, no doubt, of the extent to which we have segregated God from the mainstream of ordinary life. What, after all, makes something sacred? Sacredness rests simply in being set apart to honor God or being recognized as revealing the divine nature. God's presence makes all things—including time and space—holy, and God is present always, everywhere. All of life is holy when we recognize God's presence in it. We can celebrate even the most commonplace moments of ordinary existence as sacred.

The spiritual life is to be lived in all circumstances. Holiness is not an antiseptic state of isolation from the ordinary world. It is absolutely practical and concrete. Holy people are immersed in the dirt and sweat of real life where light and darkness contend with real consequences, for that is where God is at work. If the word I hear on Sunday has no bearing on the way I relate to my spouse, child, neighbor, or colleague; no bearing on how I make decisions, spend my resources, cast my vote, or offer my service, then my faith and my life are unrelated. The spiritual life is not one slice in a larger loaf of reality but leaven for the whole loaf.

Without such an understanding, our discussion of the centrality of family life in spiritual formation would be without foundation. If, on the other hand, we comprehend that the whole of life is intended to be a response to the gracious spirit of God's residing in and among us, we can ill afford to neglect the critical role of the family in spiritual nurture and life patterning. It is precisely among our most intimate and abiding relationships that the character of our spiritual life is not only shaped but seriously tested and revealed for what it is.

Before proceeding with our task, some clarification of terms is in order. Matters of the spirit are increasingly broadly understood in our current religious climate. What one person means by the spiritual life may bear little resemblance to what another means. Let me clarify my understanding of the terms I shall be using. The *spiritual life* as I conceive it is simply the growing life of God's spirit in us, both individually and corporately. It is like a unique dance choreographed between the Holy Spirit and the human spirit that moves us toward the truth of who we are and binds us into the great communion of love among all persons and the whole creation that lies at the very heart of God. The spiritual life is our life in grace.

Another word with increasingly wide currency is *spirituality*. While persons may use various terms to define the word, it seems consistently to point to the *way* we choose to live out our faith. Spirituality signifies a path shaped by theological convictions, patterns of life, and practices of faith that nurture our life in grace.

I understand the spiritual life to constitute the ground and goal of a particular spirituality. God's life in us is both the source and end of any given spiritual path.

For the purposes of this book, when I speak of the *spiritual life* I mean specifically the Christian spiritual life. The New Testament canon offers us a remarkable proclamation, namely that the image of the invisible God has been restored to human beings in its original beauty and clarity through Christ (Col. 1:15). Those of us who take such a teaching to heart can affirm that the work of the Holy Spirit is to conform us to the image of Christ (Col. 3:10 ff.), both as a body, the church, and as individual members of it. Then spiritual formation in a Christian theological framework means conformation to the image of Christ through the indwelling of the Holy Spirit: "And we all . . . are being changed into his likeness . . . for this comes from the Lord who is the Spirit" (2 Cor. 3:18, RSV).

When we speak as Christians of the life of God's spirit increasingly alive in us, we mean the spirit of life that animated Christ. Spiritual maturation is visible to the extent that it is "no longer I who live, but it is Christ who lives in me" (Gal. 2:20). If we can affirm this much, we will soon discover that a genuinely Christian spirituality is marked indelibly by the mystery and paradox of the cross. The shape of Christian life is uncompromisingly cruciform. "The spiritual life begins with crucifixion because at those moments we lose our illusions," notes author Parker Palmer. He goes on to point out that the cross is "necessary, inevitable, for only by dying to our false selves can the Spirit-self emerge."[2]

The process of becoming disabused of our pervasive illusions so that our authentic identity in God might emerge is one of the key potential dynamics of family interaction. What better setting can there be than a family committed to faith and to faithful relationships in which to trust letting go of false supports? What more practical setting in which to learn the blessing of the beatitudes that run so counter to our prevailing social prescriptions for happiness?

Yet allowing this potential dynamic of family life to develop is no easy task. Illusions die hard; mercy and forgiveness cannot be forced; and suffering unjustly for the sake of God's truth can seem humanly impossible. This is one reason why we need intentional spiritual practices within the home. There are other good reasons as well.

One of the most privileged and peculiarly human tasks we have inherited is that of recognizing and naming God's presence in life. Most people of faith begin that task with some deep, experiential conviction of God's reality. There are mysteries here whose origins reason does little to explain. It is safe to say simply that every experience of God's truth originates in God's gracious self-revealing.

Foundational experiences of God come in many guises. Perhaps the most mysterious is the young child's seemingly innate and untaught knowledge of God—a subject we will expand on in chapter 4. Another deeply rooted source of our experience of God's presence comes through the most significant people in our lives; we know something of God's love in the love of our parents and grandparents; our friends and teachers; our siblings, spouses, and children; and sometimes through the grace of complete strangers. The natural world can be a powerful vehicle for perceiving God's awesome presence and creativity; many people describe experiences in nature as foundational to their faith. Certainly not least, the church may be the context for one's deepest experience of God. Sometimes a congregation is the first community in which a person experiences being loved, accepted, and called to service by God.

However, it takes more than foundational experiences of God to remain adequately nourished on our spiritual pilgrimage. We are profoundly vulnerable creatures, haunted by doubts that shake our faith from every conceivable source. The tragedies and irrational evils of life assault our convictions; the secular attitudes of our culture seduce and undermine us; our tendency to become self-absorbed, distracted, and forgetful leads us away from deeper spiritual intuitions.

We seem to need continual reassurance, fresh understanding, and maturing integration in order to keep faith alive and well. Role models in our families and churches are a critical part of this support. Often a parent, a spouse, a pastor, a teacher, or even (perhaps especially!) a child has brought us back to the reality of God with renewed vitality. Such persons are mentors in the faith. The tradition and teaching of the church serve in this capacity as well, reminding us of larger truths and rerooting our confidence in God when life resembles a bad dream.

We can choose to grow into a deeper grace of union with the Christ whom we come to see, name, and love "in the flesh" of daily existence. If we consciously desire to know and love God more fully, we will be drawn to the intentional practice of spiritual disciplines.

Spiritual disciplines are like garden tools. The best hoe and rake cannot guarantee healthy fruit; they can only help create less obstructed conditions for growth. Various methods of prayer, scripture study, and discernment have the character of such tools. They can keep the soil of our love clear from obstruction and distraction, enabling us to remain more attuned to the mysterious work of God's spirit. In effect, spiritual disciplines draw us into a labor of cooperation with God—a labor whose primary expression is *receptivity*. Receiving God's word lies one step ahead of responding to the divine will. Surely a primary aim in the spiritual life is greater responsiveness to the stirrings of God's grace within and around us.

Part of our task in this book will be to discover the spiritual disciplines inherent in the very structure and nature of family life. Part will be to explore creative ways to incorporate time-honored practices into contemporary family life. Both types of discipline are means through which God may graciously transform our ingrained and self-preoccupied habits so that our foundational experiences of God's reality can mature. The beauty of such disciplines is that as we learn to offer them freely and faithfully, God works through them with still greater freedom and faithfulness to reshape us according to the mind of Christ.

If our current much-needed and sometimes desperate search for a spiritual anchor is to bear lasting fruit, we must recognize that a faithful family is our first spiritual center, one that needs to reestablish itself with every generation.

# 1

# The Family as Forming Center

~

*Every action taken, every response made, every dynamic of relationship, every thought held, every emotion allowed: these are the minuscule arenas where, bit by bit . . . we are shaped into some kind of being. . . . Life is, by its very nature, spiritual formation.*

—M. Robert Mulholland, Jr.

THE AUTHOR OF THESE WORDS reminds us that spiritual formation is not optional; it is simply "the primal reality of life."[1] As human beings fashioned in the image and likeness of God, we are innately spiritual as well as physical and psychological creatures. Forces that shape or influence any single dimension of our life inevitably affect the whole of our connected being. Because we are born or adopted into families of one sort or another and because these families of origin are the principal context of daily life and relationship during our most formative years, it seems reasonable to conclude that the family of origin is the first place of spiritual formation. For better or worse, whether intentionally or haphazardly, it is within these "given" families that, as children, our hearts and minds are fundamentally formed. Here we develop a sense of identity and heritage; here we learn patterns of relating intimately with others; here we hammer out our values, ideals, and habits day by day and year by year.

With time, the family's natural role in spiritual formation extends beyond our families of origin. Through marriage, in the raising of our own children, in relationships with extended family members including older parents, through sometimes broken and reforged marriages, our personal formation as human spiritual beings continues to unfold. Our sense of identity changes, crystallizing and recrystallizing around the shifting roles of the life cycle. Patterns of intimate relationship are impacted by one another's inviolable uniqueness; values mature; dreams are fulfilled and shattered; pain stretches us toward new growth. Life forms and re-forms us, spiritually, emotionally, and physically.

The family is not, of course, the sole context for ongoing personal formation. Life is full of alternative contexts—school, workplace, church, civic groups, the street, other cultures—in which widening circles of information and relationship continue to shape us. But those with whom we live and struggle and play most intimately have, it seems, the most enduring (even if unconscious) impact on our identity.

It is virtually impossible to overestimate the *importance* of the family to a child's total development. The basic formation of character and development of personality that occurs within the home covers all the bases: physical, emotional, mental, and spiritual. I believe that the spiritual dimension of human life is the broadest and most encompassing, the sphere within which all other dimensions of life find expression. Therefore whatever formation takes place within the home inevitably touches our spiritual lives, whether for good or for ill. That is why I believe that the family, more than any other context of life, is the foundational arena of spiritual formation for children.

I am speaking here of spiritual formation in the general and broadest sense. Christians, as for others of specific faith traditions, need a more particular focus. To New Testament scholar Robert Mulholland, Jr., "the question is not *whether* to undertake spiritual formation; the question is *what kind* of spiritual formation are we engaged in. Are we being increasingly conformed to the world, or are we being increasingly conformed to the image of Christ?" His theological premise matches the one I suggest in my introduction: "Christian spiritual formation is the process of being conformed to the image of Christ."[2]

This brings us to a few central *implications.* If parents actually are as formative for young children as we are claiming, it is only reasonable that families of faith and their church communities will want to do all they can to ensure two things:

∾First, that the kind of formation inevitably taking place within family life will be positive, life-giving, and constructive. In an era when the word *abuse* has become painfully familiar, that is a minimal level implication.

∾Second, that the spiritual formation that occurs will move family members toward the likeness of Christ and the vision of God's reign, rather than toward conformity to the values and vision of the world. In other words, that it will be *Christian* spiritual formation.

If these expectations are to be fulfilled, it will require definite *intentionality* on the part of communities of faith and their families. How can the church help its families catch on to the vision of their critical importance, and then follow through on the implications of this vision with greater intentionality?

I think families intentionally communicate the values and vision of faith in two basic ways. The first is through the *natural opportunities* of life together— occasions that simply characterize the relational fabric of family life. The second is through *intentional practices*—simple but specific structures and patterns that support the spiritual potential within families of faith.

While realizing that the growth of our life in Christ is a gradual process, we can nurture it from the moment of our birth and continue to our dying breath. The intentionality, content, and goal of Christian faith distinguish this process from the spiritual formation intrinsic to life itself. Christian spiritual formation requires conscious choice and a responsive awareness to the presence of the risen Lord in all life. I believe that families of committed Christian faith are privileged places of intentional formation in Christ—that, indeed, such families are the *primary* locus of faith formation for children and constitute a significant context for continued adult spiritual growth as well. I use the term *primary* both in the sense of *first* and of *principal.*

Let me restate unequivocally the central thesis of this book. The family, more than any other context of life, is the foundational place of spiritual formation in its broad sense, especially for children. If the church wishes to see the content of this formation as explicitly Christian, it will need to take the role and support of the family far more seriously than it has. I am an ordained minister, much concerned with the place of the congregation and of church programs in spiritual formation. Therefore my own thesis has posed significant challenges to my thinking. Over time, it has stretched my presuppositions and become increasingly cogent.

## Family Formation

Children learn what they live. They absorb knowledge of the world by what they experience and observe. We know that children learn more from what adults *do* than from what adults *say*; they are sensitive to the "hidden curriculum" behind teaching—those lessons embodied in method and structure that either reinforce or contradict the content.

For example, a teacher may talk about learning by doing when she or he is actually spoon-feeding facts into the minds of her students. If the teacher prevents experiential learning through the teaching methods employed, the child perceives that learning is a dominance-submission relationship between teacher and student and may come to distrust his or her own experience as a valuable dimension of genuine learning.

This is equally true at home! After all, the home environment is a child's first classroom for learning about others and about the world. Relationships with parents and siblings are primary and critical. Children quite unconsciously reflect their parents' feelings, values, beliefs, and living patterns—absorbing them with uncanny rapidity.

If parents speak of love and care, but there is no warmth in the home, the child is affected by the reality behind the words. Parents may instruct their children to "be nice" and proceed to throw barbs of sarcasm at each other; parents may exchange angry words but exhibit the capacity to forgive each other; single parents may complain about lack of support, yet give clear evidence that faith and hope sustain them through the additional burdens of raising children alone. In all cases, the child is most deeply shaped by the lived message: "No spoken words can convey one's truth, one's belief system, one's world view so much as these life-words lived out day by day in ordinary families."[3]

I do not wish to imply that each child is not absolutely unique, gifted from birth with certain characteristics and a distinct personality. A child is not incapable of resisting parents' perspectives and personal orientations, as every parent well knows. Nonetheless, a child is vulnerable in a deep and abiding way to the influences of the home, whether for good or for ill.

Psychologists have known for years that a child's earliest experiences with significant adults shape the whole identity in fundamental ways. The first year of life is cited as the most critical in establishing a child's basic sense of self-acceptance and capacity for intimacy. When an infant receives love and warmth, physically embodied in cradling arms, words of delight, smiling eyes, and response to physical needs, that child learns basic trust. The experience of parental love is a child's first means of receiving divine love through human channels. Parents naturally become the child's original model and image for God's character and presence.

Our childhood experience of intimate relationships within the family circle has an enormous impact later in life, not only on our capacity for intimacy with others but also with God. Pastoral counselors and spiritual directors frequently experience just how tenacious the effects of this connection can be.

A friend whose vocation is spiritual guidance and retreat work told me that when a person comes to her for the first time, she begins by asking the individual to reflect on this question: "In what ways has my experience with parents, or with emotionally significant people in my life, colored my view of what God is like and of how God relates to me?"[4] My friend has discovered that if a deep level of trust in a source of loving care and wise authority has not been experienced by a person as a child, there will likely be a long and costly struggle as the grown child learns to trust the loving wisdom of God.

The family continues to play a key role in spiritual formation long past childhood. As family configurations change with the seasons of life, they remain centers in which relationships of intimacy shape and reshape our values, ideals, and patterns of life.

Christian spirituality is primarily and essentially relational. From the standpoint of faith, the way we relate to one another must be identified as the *quintessential* spiritual discipline of family and church life. I believe it is our native vocation as Christians to reflect God's love, forgiveness, and challenge to faithful growth in whatever context we find ourselves. There is nothing abstract or easy about expressing consistent respect and care for one another, especially amid the mundane, repetitious routines and daily stresses of life together. That's what makes family spirituality such a challenge.

Dolores Leckey, head of the U.S. Bishops' Committee on the Laity, characterizes the family as "a laboratory for soul work." It is a context where we can learn, in the most practical and concrete way, to love others in their frail particularity. For the majority of us, whether we like it or not, families are our most basic communities. In them we are bound to one another by life vows, blood ties, or the complete personal commitment expressed in adoption.[5]

Families are small communities in which we receive countless opportunities to learn how to love in the nitty-gritty of daily life. Families call us to learn the way of Christ not only in the endless round of dirty dishes and diapers but in the face of broken promises and shattered trust. Family life is a crucible of intensive intimacy. The greater our love, the more vulnerable we become to pain and disappointment but the greater also our capacity for fulfillment and delight.

Since families represent our most intimate and committed relationships, they are the most obvious testing ground of our capacity to grow in love, fidelity, trust, and freedom. The character of our spiritual life is deeply shaped by our most intimate and abiding relationships, and so it is precisely among such relationships that our spiritual maturity is most seriously tested and revealed for what it is. Family life does not allow us to escape into illusions of misty-eyed, pious idealism. Within the family the difficult practicality of love demands our constant effort, through failures and victories alike.

## Family as Domestic Church

Beyond what I consider the incontrovertible psychosocial realities, there are intriguing historical antecedents to the primacy of family in spiritual formation. Pope Paul VI, in referring to the family as "domestic church," was reaching back to an ancient and time-honored tradition.[6] Edward Hays outlines the development of that tradition in the introduction to his magnificent book, *Prayers for the Domestic Church:*

> The first altar around which primitive people worshipped was the hearth, whose open fire burned in the center of the home. The next altar-shrine was the family table where meals were celebrated and great events in the personal history of the family were remembered. The priests and the priestesses of these first rituals were the fathers and mothers of families.[7]

Hays reminds us that the eldest patriarch or matriarch of the clan held the power of blessing long before the rise of an institutional priesthood. Even when temples were established, the home was considered the primal place of worship. Each home had a central, sacred place for prayer and remembrance of larger spiritual realities in daily life.

Jewish tradition and practice still express the ancient centrality of the home in worship. The Jewish faith has been characterized as a "table spirituality" in which the central feasts and holy days are celebrated around the altar of the family table. Indeed, Christians are in danger of forgetting that their holiest sacrament the Lord's Supper is a reinterpretation of the Jewish Passover—a celebration remembered in the home of each Jewish family and presided over by parents. Jesus celebrated the Passover with his chosen "family" of disciples in a home, not a synagogue; and the early Christian community continued to celebrate the Lord's Supper in one another's homes. As Christians affirmed their spiritual bond in Christ, blood ties of family and clan were relativized, but homes remained a focal gathering point for prayer and worship.

Hays contends that only with time did church buildings gradually eclipse the home as the central place of Christian worship. He suggests that "the communal church . . . was intended to be a gathering point . . . not a substitute for the domestic church, the home. Families came to the village church bringing the gifts of their . . . family prayers, and these were joined to prayers of other families to form the rich and inspiring prayer-mosaic of the Christian community."[8]

In our day, the church usually is viewed as the primary teacher of faith and the mediator of spiritual values. Theologically speaking, this is a proper perspective. The problem arises when the church is identified primarily with its structure or with its professional leadership rather than with its full membership. Specialized training is so esteemed in our culture that we have come to trust only "professionals" to teach, heal, or advise us. It is small wonder that parents often feel inadequately equipped for the demanding and challenging task of teaching children— whether about faith, sexuality, or even basic human values. More and more, the burden of such teaching has been shifted to schools and churches. Schools and churches play a significant role in shaping the values, ideals, and experiences of young people; but these institutions cannot adequately substitute for the uniquely formative home environment.

The church has consistently held that religious education begins in the home as children imitate their parents and participate in family and community worship. All other forms of education are supplements to this basic formation in faith. "No matter where you look in our Judeo-Christian heritage it is the parents who have the prime responsibility to bring up their children in the faith. It is an awesome responsibility," states renowned Christian educator John Westerhoff.[9] For all their specialized training, church professionals realize that if a child is not receiving basic Christian nurture in the home, even the best teachers and curriculum will have minimal impact. Once-a-week exposure simply cannot compete with daily experience where personal formation is concerned.

Despite the church's historic insistence on the primary role of parents in shaping their children's spiritual capacities, congregations today often fall prey to the temptation of professionalism. Many well-meaning churches have failed to offer families adequate support for the dimension of their vocation related to spiritual growth in the home. Instead the message effectively communicated is that families receive their spiritual nurture *only* at church. Yet at church, family members typically are assigned to age groups, each with specialized resources. The effect can be to undermine parents' confidence in the value of their home teaching capacities, as well as to imply that "real" Christian education is best achieved by separating family members. Ironically, even church programs on marriage and parenting are yet another means of separating parents and children in a culture where extracurricular activities for both children and adults contribute to serious fragmentation of family life.

Of course church-sponsored classes and groups in the area of family life are both necessary and helpful. But if such programs are the sole, or even predominant, means by which a church focuses attention on its families, the implication is that contemporary families are in need of "fixing" by the church or by other professionals. One subtle distortion is the assumption that there is some abstract norm for the Christian family, whose secret is known and dispensed by the church. Again the effect is disempowering for the family. It can lead people to believe that if their family is less than perfect, it is unacceptable to the church. When families feel constrained to cover their pain and brokenness in order to present the appearance of an ideal Christian family, real spiritual growth is paralyzed. In the next chapter, we will explore more fully the implications of this all-too-common phenomenon, which one of my colleagues calls "dressing up pretty for Jesus."

How can the church become the community of families and individuals that helps its member families recognize and claim God's grace in the midst of their failure and incompleteness? How can the church help families erase the assumptions and fears that inhibit them from fulfilling their primary role, instead of trying to replace the family in that role? How can the church let families know that they are loved and accepted, imperfect as they are, and that they are called to be blessed instruments of God's most critical labor: forming each person in the mind and spirit of Christ? What if the family were not merely the object of the church's teaching mission, but one of the most basic units of the church's mission to the world?

What I am suggesting is that both the "communal church" and the "domestic church" need to recapture a vision of the Christian family as a sacred community. This will require an awareness of the "sacred" in the "secular," of God in the flesh of human life. The division we assume between heaven and earth will need healing:

> What a waste it is to be surrounded by heaven, by a sky "made white by angels' wings" and to be unaware of it. . . . Yet, if we can rediscover this vision, then we too may be able to . . . let the mundane become the edge of glory, and find the extraordinary in the ordinary.

With these words, Esther de Waal encourages us "to make the busy, boring, relentless daily life tasks the basis for . . . finding the presence of God."[10]

A simple lay monk Brother Lawrence made famous the phrase, "practicing the presence of God."[11] He was speaking of a conscious awareness of God in the midst of washing dishes, preparing meals, and having conversations in the community that was his "family." Evelyn Underhill writes of "practical mysticism" in much the same vein, referring to the art of seeing Reality in common, daily realities.[12] Family life is an arena in which most of us have natural occasion to "practice" God's presence— to learn the discipline of keeping our eyes open to the divine Reality shining through our most ordinary moments.

Do you believe that God is present in the smile of a child, in the tears of a parent's grief over a suffering adolescent, in the sudden breakthrough of understanding between quarreling spouses? Eternal truths can be learned by observing the most common elements of life: nursing an infant may be a window onto God's nurturing care for each of us,[13] bandaging a cut can help us know the healing desire of God; playing games may speak of the divine playfulness that knows our need for recreation; tending a garden may teach us the dynamics of growth. Families learn that they are sacred communities when they begin to name and claim the many forms of God's grace in their daily life.

If the family is to take its spiritual vocation seriously, it will need to be intentional about recovering old ways and creating new ways to grow together in faith. There are some helpful starting points. With what images of God are family members operating—Santa Claus? the boss? security guard in the sky? the great physician? father or mother? child? shepherd? ocean? wind? light? What are the central stories of scripture that shape the faith understanding of each member and of the family as a whole? Images of God may change and scriptural foundations be reinterpreted as the family grows.

Simple structures, symbols, and rituals are important means of growth. What faith rituals and spiritual disciplines will a family choose to celebrate? What forms of family decision making might best allow God's will to be discerned and followed? How will family members hold one another accountable in their discipleship without resorting to authoritarian legalism or guilt-inspiring moralism? How do family members help one another discover their natural gifts for service and develop their talents for mission?

All of these questions and more may be the fodder of family reflection and discussion. How a given family chooses to respond to such questions is a matter for prayerful discernment and can take a rich variety of forms. No single path can be mapped out because each family, like each individual, is unique. But intentionality and choice are crucial to all families who wish to fulfill their calling as a primary vehicle of spiritual formation in the body of Christ. As families make choices about life patterns that nurture spiritual growth in the home, they will become increasingly conscious of the grace of being sacred communities.

## *For Reflection*

～What is your response to the idea that the family is the primary place of spiritual formation?

～ How has your own family experience formed you spiritually?

～How would you describe the role of the church in your spiritual nurture?

～Do you ever experience the church as divisive of family? If so, how?

～In what ways do you experience the church as supportive of the spiritual vocation of the family?

# 2

# The Family as Earthen Vessel

～

*For it is the God who said, "Let light shine out of dark-ness," who has shone in our hearts to give the light of the knowledge of the glory of God in the face of Christ. But we have this treasure in earthen vessels, to show that the tran-scendent power belongs to God and not to us. We are af-flicted in every way, but not crushed; perplexed, but not driven to despair . . . always carrying in the body the death of Jesus, so that the life of Jesus may also be manifested in our bodies.*

—2 Corinthians 4:6-8, 10; RSV

OF WHAT ARE WE ACTUALLY SPEAKING when we discuss the family? The assumption underlying our common usage of the word takes for its norm the nuclear family unit. To most North Americans, a "traditional family" means a husband and a wife with the children of their union. For years this ideal structure has been merged with traditional male-female role distinctions in which the husband was understood to be "breadwinner" and the wife "homemaker."

In the current cultural climate, we encounter several diffi-culties with this traditional family image. The ideal that domi-nated the cultural imagination of the 1950s—the two-child family with station wagon and dog—is a vanishing species in our society and simply does not reflect the diverse reality of family life today.

There is indeed a sociological primacy to the nuclear family that derives from patriarchal or matriarchal lineage in various human cultures, but the reduction of *households* to purely nuclear family units seems to be a relatively recent historical phenomenon—largely expressive of Western societies. Even in the United States, what we call the "extended family" has been a norm of household life far longer than the nuclear family. Grandparents and single aunts or uncles were perhaps most typical of the relatives who lived together with parents and children in comprising a single household, a family pattern that persisted well into the twentieth century. With World War II, a new mobility emerged, tied to the military and related industries. Families relocated at an even greater pace after the war as job markets continued to open beyond small-town parameters. The close-knit fabric of extended families, which depended on geographical proximity, was irreparably torn. Extended families became "expanded" families, spreading across state lines nationwide and even across national boundaries.

A general correlation exists between economic prosperity and reduction of the scope of households in the United States. As family income increases, relatives beyond the nuclear unit tend to establish and maintain their own residences, an expression of the autonomy and individual freedom so prized in North American culture. As family income declines, extended family grouping becomes more of an economic necessity.

This correlation might seem to explain why extended family life is more prevalent among certain ethnic groups in the United States, such as those of Hispanic and Southeast Asian origin. Yet while economic hardship may be pertinent to a certain extent, such groups often embody cultural values in which extended family structure is the desirable norm. I observe that values of wider kinship solidarity and mutual cooperation are stronger among many American ethnic groups, including some persons of European immigrant backgrounds.

The situation among African-American families is greatly complicated by our shameful history of slavery and racial prejudice. Native Africans, from whom much of our African-American populace is descended, brought their own patterns of kinship from diverse cultural and tribal affiliations with them to this country. Some kinship structures were patrilineal; some were matrilineal; a few were of double descent. All placed a primary value on extended family relationships.

These kinship patterns were disrupted systematically by the institution of slavery. Both adults and children were sold without regard to blood or marriage ties. For years slave traders favored young men, and African-American females were extremely scarce. Even when this imbalance was redressed, however, marriage among slaves was not recognized either by church or state. "There was . . . an absence of legal foundation, sanction, and protection of marriage as an institution among slaves. Slave women were exploited by white owners, overseers, and their sons for pleasure and profit. A role for the African-American man as husband and father was systematically denied. Families were willfully separated by selling members to different plantations. The African-American family had no physical, psychological, social, or economic protection."[1]

Under such circumstances, mutual affection and support among groups of slaves often became constitutive of "family" in a broad sense. Children born into slavery were "out of wedlock" by virtue of the institution itself. They were informally adopted into symbolic families not limited by blood ties. This resilient response to the disruption of natural kinship is still practiced in economically depressed African-American communities where widespread illegitimacy reflects "the lengthening shadow of slavery."[2]

What is remarkable is that even within the dehumanizing institution of slavery, natural family structures survived in this modified form. Although the nuclear family appeared to have disintegrated, the extended family—often with strong maternal nurture—became vital. Some African-American scholars perceive the figure of the grandmother to be especially influential in both family and church.[3] The African-American church has been a powerful ally for the African-American family, consistently strengthening the bonds of extended family solidarity within the African-American community.

Middle-class white Americans have experienced some return to a modified extended family in the form of adult children who care for elderly parents, often in their own homes. A variety of factors account for this resurgence. First, with better medical care people are living longer. "The graying of America" is a social iceberg whose tip we have only begun to see. It is estimated by the U.S. Bureau of the Census that the number of persons over 80 years of age will increase by 95 percent between 1980 and 2000. With the same circumstances, the number of persons 85 and over was expected to rise between 91 percent (medium projection) and 100 percent (high projection).[4] Not only are our retirement centers and nursing homes strained by sheer numbers, but the cost of providing care through such facilities is rapidly becoming prohibitive. Fortunately more than mere economics has contributed to the increase of home care for the elderly. Most Americans still believe that primary responsibility for older parents belongs to family members. Although large numbers of persons over 65 live alone (79 percent of whom are women),[5] up to 80–90 percent of care received by the elderly is given by family members (also predominantly female).[6]

The difficulties in defining the family according to traditional norms becomes more evident as we look at current statistics:

～Fewer than 7 percent of families today are composed of a married couple with two children where the husband is sole provider (the stereotypical norm of the 1950s and early 1960s).[7]

～Only 54.8 percent of all U.S. households in 1994 were married-couple families, compared to 70.6 percent in 1970.[8]

～Only 25.8 percent of all U.S. households in 1986 were comprised of married couples with children.[9]

～Twenty-six percent of all children in the U.S. in 1993 lived in one-parent families. Eighty-five percent were headed by females (20.9 percent of white children, 57.1 percent of

African-American children, 31.8 percent of Hispanic children).[10]

～As of 1993, one in two marriages ended in divorce.[11]

～In 1993, both spouses were employed in 59.1 percent of families comprised of married couples with children, up from 32.8 percent in 1976. In 1990, 59.7 percent of mothers with children under the age of six were in the work force.[12]

～In 1993, 24.5 percent of all household were composed of persons living alone. This is an increase of 118 percent since 1970. Forty percent of persons living alone are 65 or older.[13]

～In 1992, 24.2 percent of all births were to unwed mothers.[14]

Given the inadequacy of stereotypes, how are we to define family? The Census Bureau defines a family household as "two or more persons related by birth, marriage, or adoption and residing together."[15] Some 87 percent of the U.S. population qualifies for family life by these criteria.[16] Craig Dykstra suggests "a common sense definition": "'Family' is that group of persons with whom we are linked as parents or children or siblings or spouses or kin, by birth, by adoption, or by marriage."[17] By this definition, everyone is a family member. William Sheek offers a structural definition of the family within the framework of faith: "We, as sisters and brothers in the family of God, accept equally as families those who are related by marriage or remarriage, blood or adoption; those who covenant to live together as family; and those single persons and persons living alone who choose to be family with others outside their kinship families."[18] To distinguish between family and household is important here; a household may be comprised of a single person who is related to a wider family.

Although family configurations vary widely, eminent sociologist Robert Bellah accords "a certain priority, sociologically and ethically, to the family defined as husband, wife, and children."[19] Without denying the more broadly inclusive definitions of family—those who reside in one household or those who "feel like family" to one another—there remains a historical, sociological, and biological significance in the particular kinship arrangement of a married man and woman with children. While recognizing that "there can be a kind of family where people are committed to one another . . . without fitting this central, normative definition," Bellah nonetheless wishes "to reassert the centrality and special dignity of what we call the traditional, or nuclear, family."[20] Even in extended family structures, relationships are ordered with reference to this central nucleus: the basic triad of father, mother, and child.

Bellah seems to be suggesting that there is a normative character to the nuclear family unit. Even though it no longer represents a statistical norm in the United States (married households without children have predominated over those with children since 1980),[21] the nuclear family remains biologically and sociologically normative. Such a norm gives a reference point for understanding the multitude of existing variations on the family theme; it does not imply a devaluation of those variations.

The centrality of this essential family unit is reflected in our language of Christian faith as well. Language describing nuclear family relationships has been used metaphorically to describe spiritual relationships. Thus, although the claim of Christ on a disciple relativizes the claims of the kinship family, believers become a new "family" in the household of God. Familial biblical images include our being "adopted children" of God and "brothers and sisters" in Christ, who is sometimes called "our elder brother."

In the Roman Catholic and Eastern Orthodox traditions, God is understood to be our spiritual father, while the church universal—of which Mary the mother of Jesus is seen as archetype—becomes our spiritual mother. Many Protestants who would not affirm a theology of Mother Mary are nonetheless distressed at the predominance of masculine imagery—father, son, or brother—in our language of spiritual kinship. For increasing numbers, the solution is to incorporate feminine identity into the deity. Feminist theology affirms that the image of God, in which both male and female are created, must encompass both masculine and feminine dimensions to reflect the fullness of God. Therefore to invoke God as mother is simply to recognize the feminine side of the Holy One.

It is striking to me that both ancient and modern solutions to balancing the masculine and feminine in faith language suggest our profound attraction to that core expression of human relationships embodied in man, woman, and child. As children of God, we feel a deeply rooted need for both father and mother.

It seems reasonable then to affirm an honored place in human society for the archetypal expression of family represented in the traditional model. While affirming that the wide variety of mutually committed relationships prevalent in our society can legitimately be spoken of as family, our primary concern in this book is a particular expression of family—that unit of intimate relationships whose nexus is the nurture of children. Whether the children are biological or adopted; whether the parent figures are married, single, stepparents, foster parents, grandparents, or other relatives acting in the parental role; whether the structure is nuclear or extended, we are concerned primarily to indicate those ways in which family life is of critical importance in the spiritual formation of children and to encourage practices whereby the intention and content of that formation explicitly reflect Christian life and faith. In addition, many of the dynamics described in this book apply to the ongoing formation of adults in families. Although I have chosen not to develop these, I would encourage readers to draw out implications and make connections wherever possible.

## Families Made of Clay

The image of the traditional family perhaps remains stronger in churches than any other segment of North American society. Many churches project a clear, if unspoken, expectation that Christian families will adhere to an ideal norm. What it means to be a Christian family will depend largely on the way a given church or denomination interprets scriptural references to family life.

It may be instructive to look at the institution of marriage as a specific case in point, since it is the constitutive foundation of family in a normative sense. The few teachings of Jesus concerning marriage recorded in the Gospels indicate that he understood the marriage bond to be permanent in this life (Mark 10:6-

9) and that he took divorce to be an extremely serious matter (Mark 10:11-12; Luke 16:18). Yet even Jesus allowed that "unchastity" was grounds for legitimate divorce (according to Matt. 5:32; 19:9). Paul, who followed Jesus' stricter teachings on marriage, conceded that when believers and unbelievers were married, divorce was acceptable if the unbeliever so desired (1 Cor. 7:15).

The church as a whole shares the expectation that a man and a woman who choose to unite in the bond of marriage do so with a full commitment to remain married for life. The wording of traditional marriage rites makes the solemnity and sacredness of this vow clear. It is a life promise made before God and the community of faith, intended to reflect Christ's faithful love for the church. Yet we humans are frail in our capacity to sustain even our most sacred vows; we fail in living out our best-intended promises. The church's response to that failure has been varied. Sometimes it has forbidden divorce and refused to recognize broken marriage as a grievous breach in need of the healing, reconciling power of God's spirit in the church. Sometimes, while grudgingly acknowledging the reality of human failure in marriage, it has stigmatized divorced persons and their families as failed Christians or even failed human beings.

At the other end of the spectrum, we have witnessed among a minority of clergy a uniquely contemporary response: diluting the language of wedding vows to accommodate the ambivalent expectations (and sometimes less-than-serious intent) between partners queasy about marriage, presumably hoping to assuage the harmful consequences of guilt should the marriage crumble.

I find the theology of the Eastern Orthodox church particularly illuminating on this issue. Orthodox theology has long held that marriage is a sacrament in the sense of "mystery" (see Eph. 5:32). A Christian marriage is to reveal something of the purpose for which we are created, which is to participate in the kingdom of God. When a man and a woman become "one flesh" out of love for each other, it is understood as a reflection of God's choice to become one flesh with us out of the infinite and eternal divine love. Christian marriage then is set within the context of the Incarnation. Christ, the incarnate Lord, is joined to his "bride," the church, sacramentally. Therefore, marriage in the Orthodox tradition is inconceivable apart from the eucharistic feast, which is understood to be a participation in the reality of God's kingdom.

Yet the capacity for a man and a woman to participate in this eternal expression of God's love can only be a gift of grace. Unearned grace is the essence of the sacrament, for lifetime vows of faithfulness are impossible to make out of mere human willpower. There are times and circumstances where, because of human sin, the grace implied by marriage has not been received or has not been brought to fruition. If, after serious effort and counsel, the bond remains destructive rather than life-giving, the church finds it appropriate to recognize that a marriage does not, in fact, exist; that is, the grace of its nature as sacrament is not present. Under these circumstances, while not encouraging remarriage, the church will issue permission to remarry if it is desired.[22]

In essence, the Eastern Orthodox church understands divorce as a grave expression of human sin but provides means for repentance and opportunity for new beginnings. For centuries the Orthodox perspective stood in stark contrast to the legalistic Roman Catholic doctrine of "indissolubility" in marriage, which could not tolerate divorce theologically except under the most extreme circumstances and would not permit remarriage until a spouse's death. Roman Catholic doctrine since Vatican II has made broader provision for marriage annulment.

It would be impossible to estimate how many thousands of divorced Christians have left the church because of overt rejection or judgmental avoidance within their congregations. Following often lengthy and anguished divorces, these wounded members of the body are deeply in need of the love and healing care of the entire church. And for those who have custody of children, even after the worst wounds have healed, a great need for sensitivity to the increased burdens of single parenting remains.

Divorce is by no means the only form of brokenness that makes families feel unworthy in the church. The second half of

Tolstoy's celebrated phrase seems to apply here: "Happy families are all alike; every unhappy family is unhappy in its own way."[23] Family misery does take a bewildering range of shapes in our day. Couples may be living under conditions of extreme stress; although remaining married, their life together is marred by constant friction and sometimes accompanied by emotional or physical abuse. Parents may feel enormous guilt when a teenage child is discovered to have been experimenting with sex, alcohol, or drugs. Yet alcohol and drug abuse is rampant among many adults as well, and sexual infidelity in marriage is a well-documented, if unhappy, reality in American life. The anguish of eating disorders has received considerable attention of late, as has the previously taboo subject of sexual abuse within families.

What seems to have proved exceptionally hard for the church to accept is that every one of these problems exists among its larger membership. We are reluctant to acknowledge just how widespread the destructive patterns of living in our culture are, all of which contribute to the deteriorating fabric of family life.

The majority of church families may be spared extreme expressions of this brokenness, but each will have its inevitable problems. Some may be no more than a phase of poor communication or a period of such frenetic busyness that all sense of togetherness vanishes. Some may surface through a crisis with a particular child who is withdrawn or belligerent or doing poorly in school. Some may be precipitated by the loss of a job, the unwelcome prospect of a move, or an anxiety-provoking medical diagnosis. A learning disability, an unyielding conflict with relatives, physical impairment, chronic illness or depression, grief over the death of a loved one—these are some of the difficulties that confront families and cause them to feel deficient and publicly unpresentable.

As mentioned earlier, families often feel that their brokenness is unacceptable at church. They may try to cover their pain and sense of failure in order to project the image of the Christian family they think the church requires of them. Dressing in "Sunday best" is a metaphor for the effort many families make to present themselves as acceptable in the presence of other church-goers, who frequently are perceived as perfect models.

Unfortunately, in hiding their real needs from the church, families may try to hide their wounds from God too. The very community where we are called to encounter and be encountered by a God of grace—a God who is holy yet merciful and who desires to heal all our diseases (Ps. 103:3)—can become a place of avoidance. If the church is not a community in which our brokenness can be acknowledged honestly, neither will it be a community in which healing takes place.

It is crucial then for churches to communicate that there is no such thing as a "perfect Christian family," any more than there is such a thing as a "perfect Christian" in this life. Because Christian families are simply families made up of individual Christians, what applies to one applies to the whole. All of us are earthen vessels—cracked, chipped, and sometimes quite broken. The greatest saints among us have been those most acutely aware of their human frailty and most free to admit it. As one of my colleagues once quipped in dead earnest, we have "clay feet right up to our necks!"[24]

But the good news is precisely that "while we still were sinners Christ died for us" (Rom. 5:8). The core of the gospel is that God loves us even in the midst of our brokenness and is always ready to confront, heal, and nurture us back to wholeness. The grace of Christian experience is always a grace at the very heart of what is broken. Jesus lived and proclaimed a peculiar message to the "perfect Jews" of his day. Answering the indignant questions of the scrupulously law-abiding Pharisees, he said, "Those who are well have no need of a physician, but those who are sick; I have come to call not the righteous but sinners" (Mark 2:17). Others have aptly noted that the church has more than its share of latter-day Pharisees who are more concerned with the appearance of blameless moral behavior than with weightier matters of mercy and authentic humility.

## God Chooses What Is Weak

Families need to understand that God loves and accepts them as they are now, with all their pain and failure. We are not speaking here of what Dietrich Bonhoeffer called "cheap grace," the abuse of God's mercy to justify sin. We are affirming that only from the foundational experience of divine grace can healing and needed forms of restoration occur. The church needs to communicate good news in the midst of family brokenness and to be a community of grace where the common wounds of our human condition can be bound up and new energy for ministry released.

Two aspects involved in this ministry of the church to families deserve particular attention: the first resembles the function of a hospital; the second involves encouragement and support for the vital mission that only families can fulfill.

The church is called to be a community that witnesses to the values and behaviors of God's kingdom and is therefore a refuge from the destructive values and behaviors of the surrounding culture. If the church is true to its calling, it will help its members learn how to live in the world but not of it (see John 17:15-16). The values of the world—wealth, power, prestige, physical beauty or prowess—are very seductive but ultimately illusory. They have no power to fulfill our deepest needs and great power to damage us not only spiritually but emotionally and even physically. We now recognize that entire families often operate as codependent systems, unconsciously reinforcing one member's destructive behavior so that the whole web of relationships becomes unhealthy. Both individuals and families need the church to proclaim and embody God's healing grace for the wounds inevitably inflicted by compulsive attachment to worldly values.

Yet the church is by no means simply a hospital ward, a place where battle-scarred Christians come to get patched up. Much current church programming for families is geared to crisis intervention, marriage counseling, and parenting aid. It occurs to me that families could easily begin to perceive themselves as trauma victims in continual need of emergency treatment. I do not wish to minimize the increasingly vital importance of such programs in view of the unprecedented stresses facing families today. Still, they constitute only one dimension of the church's ministry with families.

The role the church needs to recognize and recover in relation to its member families is that of facilitator. The church could begin by calling families to their own sense of blessed and significant identity. Christian families are instruments of God's spirit, vehicles of grace to one another within the home. Although each family is imperfect, God has gracious designs for its life and growth within the church as well as remarkable ministries for it to embody. It would be appropriate for the church to remind its families that "God chose what is weak in the world to shame the strong" (1 Cor. 1:27). So even if one's family is weakened by death, divorce, physical disability, emotional problems, or economic hardship, that family is still a living cell in the body of Christ with a mission and purpose only it has the gifts to fulfill. Each family, with its unique configuration, has special gifts for the upbuilding of the body. Christian families, like the individual Christians of which they are comprised, are "simultaneously sinners and justified" (to use Luther's signature phrase). This means that they too have a high calling to pursue.

John of the Cross, a sixteenth-century soul friend of Teresa of Avila, reportedly observed, "God has so ordained things that we grow in faith only through the frail instrumentality of one another." His words express a profound truth about human life in general and Christian life in particular. We are truly frail creatures with willing spirits and weak flesh who will the good and do the very things we abhor (see Rom. 7:13-25). Yet Paul reminds us that "we have this treasure [the life of Christ] in earthen vessels, to show that the transcendent power belongs to God and not to us" (2 Cor. 4:7, RSV). Families who cherish their faith are precisely such earthen vessels. Their members become frail instruments to one another and to those beyond the family circle for such growth in wisdom and grace as God graciously ordains.

## *For Reflection*

~How do you define family?

~What is the place of extended family in your experience?

~Explain your theology of marriage.

~How do you experience your family as an "earthen vessel"?

# 3

# Challenges
# to the Vision

~

*They will look to the earth, but will see only distress and*
*darkness. . . . The earth dries up and withers. . . . The earth*
*lies polluted under its inhabitants; for they have trans-*
*gressed laws, violated the statutes, broken the everlasting*
*covenant. Therefore a curse devours the earth, and its in-*
*habitants suffer for their guilt.*

—Isaiah 8:22; 24:4, 5-6

THE FAMILY IS UNDER SIEGE in today's society. The assault is little short of spectacular, mounted as it is from all sides. Some attacks are direct and self-evident, such as those associated with drug and alcohol abuse, teen pregnancy, and the accompanying threat of sexually transmitted disease. Poverty and low social status, disproportionately borne by women and children, can leave family members vulnerable not only to external stresses but also to all manner of self-destructive behaviors. Equally dangerous are the subtle and indirect attacks that come pleasantly packaged for middle- and upper-income family consumption. It is here, among the ubiquitous cultural messages of materialism, individualism, and competition that the essence of family life is corroded.

We might begin with the more obvious evils assailing our sense of security and order. The words of Isaiah concerning a people thoroughly enmeshed in sin have an eerily contemporary ring in our day. We live in an era filled with new forms of darkness that can make the prospect of parenting especially frightening.

To begin with, young people are very sensitive to the threats looming over our civilization. It is a well-documented fact that children today fear the threat of nuclear annihilation, as well as the threat of ecological destruction. If adults feel overwhelmed and numbed by such prospects, it is small wonder that children feel helpless despair at the state of an adult world over which they perceive themselves to have little influence.

Drug use can be a response to the conviction among many youngsters that they have no future worth preserving. For many inner city youth, the lack of prospects for decent education, jobs, or homes closes the door on hope for the future. The ubiquity of the deadly cocaine derivative "crack" makes experiments in self-destruction easier than ever. We have already noted that nearly 25% of all births in this country are to unmarried mothers.[1] We also know that about 15% of all newborns have been exposed to illegal drugs through their mothers' use.[2]

Teenage pregnancy is of more concern than ever to parents since the advent of AIDS in the United States. The fact that it can be transmitted through heterosexual as well as homosexual intimacy puts far greater numbers of young people at risk. Because of its exponential rate of increase and incurability at present, AIDS has shifted attention away from less serious but more prevalent forms of sexually transmitted disease that are reaching epidemic proportions today. Such factors can generate enormous family anxiety as children become more prone to peer pressure than to parental influence.

Peer pressure has been blamed for many of the destructive behaviors of teenagers—smoking, abusing alcohol and drugs, becoming sexually promiscuous, driving at dangerous speeds, eating prodigious quantities of junk food, indulging in frivolous fads and fashions, and even mutually encouraging despair, which has, in tragic instances, led to suicide pacts among teens. I certainly would not argue with the perception that peer influence can be destructive; yet it seems to me that much teen behavior is simply a reflection of the destructive side of current Western culture in general and of North American culture in particular.

Psychiatrist Gerald May believes that addiction is the quintessential disease of the human race. By describing it as "the most powerful psychic enemy of humanity's desire for God,"[3] May suggests that addiction is a remarkably apt rendering of sin, understood as that which separates us from God. He documents many patterns of addictive behavior whose common denominator is uncontrollable attachment. Inordinate need for security, control, possessions, approval; excessive attachment to work, ideology, consumption—all these and more can express addictive behavior as surely as can overeating, smoking, and abusing drugs or alcohol. Compulsive eating disorders such as anorexia and bulimia are addictive in nature, as are fad diets—particularly popular among women in a society that equates slenderness with beauty.

The prevalence among Americans of what could well be termed an unconscious death wish, revealed in self-destructive behavior, finds its roots in much broader, mainstream cultural attitudes and values. We must be prepared to look honestly at the devastating toll these widely accepted habits and mores are taking on our population. The pretty packaging of "the good life" we so desire is wrapped securely around the ugly elements of our culture we so fear.

## Cultural Values

It seems to me that superficiality, despair, and violence run like undercurrents through North American culture, not so much *despite* our national economic achievements as *because* of them. Our free market economy tends toward a life centered in consumerism, where personal goals are often determined by economic and technological advances. When we look at the values espoused by advertising and promoted through the popular media, we see that they characterize a ruthless arena in which people compete for wealth, status, and success through every conceivable means of manipulation and coercion. Although various levels of government can, and do to some extent, mitigate the excesses of a purely consumer-driven society, we often find public servants controlled by the same money and power values that motivate individuals in the marketplace.

These values are communicated clearly to children, even when their families resist such values. It should come as no surprise to people of faith that giving primary meaning to wealth, status, and power leads almost inevitably to despair and violence. Not only can very few live in the manner to which pop stars and sports heroes have become accustomed, but experience suggests (and our spiritual tradition confirms) that those who do usually sell their souls for the privilege. Wealth and status can leave us spiritually impoverished in countless ways. The despair that grows from trying to find ultimate meaning in decidedly nonultimate realities (a reasonable definition of idolatry) should be clear to us from the evidence of wrecked lives among the rich and famous.

Moreover, for those who cannot find legitimate means to secure "the American dream," the quick road to riches often presents itself with irresistible allure—the path of gambling, theft, drug pushing, fraud, or extortion. For the less aspiring, these may simply be desperate attempts to survive; but for many, the end justifies the means when it comes to acquiring what our culture proclaims "good."

## The Impact of Individualism

Closely related to the malaise of our technologically and materially advanced society is the individualism that characterizes much of the Western world. A decade ago, one book in particular, *Habits of the Heart*, stimulated avid conversation concerning the socially debilitating effects of North American individualism. Written by Robert Bellah in collaboration with four colleagues, the book's central thesis could be summed up as follows.

Individual needs and desires are significantly valued over social and public commitment in our nation, to the increasing detriment of all forms of social cohesion and integration. In a democratic republic, the survival of free institutions depends primarily on the extent of private citizen involvement in the public sphere. We are rapidly losing the will for such broad-based citizen participation, as cultural values focus more and more on personal fulfillment. Personal commitments are now typically justified in one of two ways: (1) utilitarian fulfillment—essentially "what I get out of it" in terms of gaining success, advantage, and/or status; and (2) expressive fulfillment—"how it makes me feel" in terms of meeting my emotional or relational needs.

A language for describing personal commitments based on the common good rather than individual fulfillment has virtually disappeared from our national vocabulary. Bellah and his associates find this a dangerous trend undermining the very foundation of what Americans most cherish—democratic freedom: "In the civic republican tradition, public life is built upon the second languages and practices of commitment that . . . [make] each individual aware of his [or her] reliance on the larger society. They form those habits of the heart that are the matrix of a moral ecology."[4] Those last two words suggest that the authors see, in the erosion of human ties, long-term consequences of the destruction of the social environment, a dynamic that directly parallels the destruction of our natural ecology.

Virtually every social unit of our culture has committed what our country's founders considered "the cardinal sin: we have put our own good, as individuals, as groups, as a nation, ahead of the common good."[5] Reflecting on the book's message, Bellah summarizes, "When we have to express everything that's loving and caring and socially responsible in terms of 'what it does for me,' that begins to undercut the very nature of those practices."[6] In moving toward radical individualism, both our social order *and* our personal identity are profoundly weakened; each depends on the other for its genuine strength.

The central findings of this book have enormous implications for family life in our culture. The entire fourth chapter is devoted to assessing individualism's harmful impact on the institution of marriage. Expressive individualism (one of the two streams of language noted above) has been fed by a widely accepted therapeutic orientation. The authors of *Habits of the*

*Heart* suggest that the therapeutic outlook "sees social life as an arrangement for the fulfillment of the needs of individuals."[7] They also believe that "in its pure form, the therapeutic attitude denies all forms of obligation and commitment in relationship, replacing them only with the ideal of full, open, honest communication among self-actualized individuals."[8]

According to the therapeutic model, the central virtue of an intimate relationship is not love but communication, on which love depends. The goal of relationship is self-fulfillment, upon which mutual fulfillment depends. One of the primary means of this goal is "self-validation," implying a certain level of independence from anyone else's standards. In a marriage based on the therapeutic worldview,

> The individual must find and assert his or her true self because this self is the only source of genuine relationships to other people. External obligations, whether they come from religion, parents, or social conventions, can only interfere with the capacity for love and relatedness. Only by knowing and ultimately accepting one's self can one enter into valid relationships with other people.[9]

There seems to be an unspoken assumption in what we might call "therapeutic ideology" that some integrated "self" exists in isolation, waiting to be uncovered by therapy. One might well ask how we can come to know our "self" apart from committed relationships with others. The purely therapeutic orientation raises other questions as well. Can love between "self-actualized persons" coexist with the practice of self-sacrifice? Are all expressions of ego restraint, all capacity to put another's needs before one's own, to be judged emotionally destructive? I am not alone in believing that there is a place for self-denial in marriage as in any committed relationship. There is a need for love expressed in action, not merely in feelings; and there is a vital function for will and intention, which transcend changing experiences of fulfillment.

Most therapists would probably acknowledge the balancing function of will, intention, and action in the work of establishing creative and mature relationships. They know, as do the best spiritual guides, that a person must be reasonably secure in feelings of self-esteem before it makes sense to ask for self-sacrifice. But establishing a secure sense of self-worth and elevating self-fulfillment to the ultimate goal of life are of two different orders. I believe, with many others, that the rise of excessive individualism in our nation has harmed the stability of marriage and family life.

## Competition and Violence

As we have shifted from community to individual values, we have tended to elevate individual rights and freedoms over the rights of the society and the common good. Our attitudes contrast strikingly with those of traditional cultures in which personal sacrifice for the sake of social cohesion is regarded as the norm. But even with reference solely to our own society, it seems there has been an evolution of American ideals over the course of some two hundred years.

There has always been a virile strain of rugged individualism in this nation's development. Stories of lone immigrants, pioneers, explorers, and cowboys have long been viewed as expressions of the archetypal American experience, imbuing individualism with near mythic qualities. Yet the framers of the U.S. Constitution understood that respect for individual liberties needed to be balanced with safeguards for the welfare of the social order. Thus, they carefully conceived and finely tuned the structure of our democratic political process. Today we are witnessing an unprecedented lack of participation by United States citizens in the political processes available to them. While the reasons for this phenomenon are complex, it could, by outward appearances, be interpreted as evidence that concern for the common welfare was more reflective of American character in the earlier phases of its history than it is now.

Elevating individual desires over the needs of the social order fosters competition over cooperation. Competition is the byword of a free-market system. Industries compete with one another for natural resources; businesses compete for economic viability; agricultural giants displace small and midsized family farms; manufacturers compete through advertising for our purchasing power. The same dynamic characterizes our education system: "Students are made to compete with one another . . . so that only the fittest and smartest will survive."[10] The author of these words notes with sadness that cooperative modes of learning in the classroom are actively discouraged, even viewed with suspicion as barely disguised forms of cheating. As a result, many "well-educated" people in our culture who are formed by conventional pedagogy are ill-suited to help create the kind of social cohesion and community life we so desperately need.

With the proper attitude, competition can be a positive dynamic that motivates us to achieve the best of which we are capable. Given our mixed motives, however, it frequently becomes a cover for aggression, self-aggrandizement, or the control of others. If becoming "number one" is of paramount importance, as the creed of competition implies, then it is a relatively small step to assume that any means of getting to the top is legitimate. The extent to which businesses are engaged in outmaneuvering, overpowering, and even belittling their competition is alarming testimony to the destructive streak in this "all-American" way of life.

Closer to home, when children feel forced to compete for what they perceive to be the scarce rewards of adult praise and approval, we should not be surprised if they become angry, envious, suspicious, and resentful toward one another. Experience suggests to me that competition is often the socially acceptable handmaid of hostility and violence.

One further characteristic of modern society that has had significant consequences for the family is the compartmentalization of life. The explosion of scientific and technological know-how has resulted inevitably in specialties, even subspecialties. We need experts for everything now, from fixing our computer-tuned cars to fixing our cholesterol-clogged hearts. We call upon professionals to direct us in every sphere. Although this perception is changing, for decades we have been ingrained with the decrees of popular wisdom: "Doctor knows best" or "Leave decisions to those who have the inside information." Many corporations fear changing direction without consulting professional forecasters. In such an environment, consultants have proliferated. We have tax consultants, career consultants, and fitness consultants—not to mention a whole range of professionals trained to advise us on emotional stress and relational problems. The same kind of thinking leads many to prefer school over family as the locus of values education or to lay the entire burden of Christian education at the feet of church professionals.

My point is simply that in our complex modern world, we tend to rely on specialized resources to solve our problems. We no longer feel confident in the general knowledge and common-sense solutions that grow out of our connections and mutual commitments as ordinary people.

## Secular and Sacred Contrasted

Over the disintegrating fabric of our social life looms the dense shadow of secularism. We do not live in an era that cherishes a consciousness of the holy. Despite the religious motto on our national coins, we have become so pluralistic and idiosyncratic in our beliefs that we can no longer claim a common faith in God a recent phenomenon in the history of the Western world Science and technology can provide a sufficient worldview for some, and the reduction of faith to ethical living seems adequate for others. Disciplines such as psychology, sociology, and anthropology are equally capable of reducing religion to purely human categories. Our education has become thoroughly secular in the service of one of our guarantors of individual freedom: the separation of church and state.

For the sake of tolerance, it is important to safeguard the right of all people to follow the dictates of conscience and to protect them from the imposition of any single vision of truth. That is part of the genius of a free society. It is also important, as people of faith, to recognize the price we pay for these safeguards. Only private institutions—families, churches, synagogues, and private schools that receive no government funding—have the right to teach a practicing faith. Life lived in relation to any genuine sense of the presence of God is absent from the culture at large. Consciousness of the holy has effectively been reduced to the private sphere. The sacredness of life is scarcely visible in the public sphere except in the most general and nonreligious terms. If life lived in conscious relationship to the divine presence is also lost from family life, as it has been to a large extent, the sphere of awareness of the holy is constricted further. Our culture needs the witness of families and individuals of committed faith.

The thoroughgoing secularity of our attitudes is perhaps nowhere more clearly revealed than in our Western way of life. We have treated the whole created order as an object to satisfy our insatiable craving for goods and pleasure. The earth's resources have been plundered and indiscriminately poisoned for the sake of corporate profit and consumer satisfaction. We seem comfortable with the astonishing illusion that we deserve ever-higher standards of living. We have arrogantly assumed our lifestyle to be the model for developing countries, as if those countries had no models of value to us and as if the earth could sustain our standard of life for its entire human population. We have looked upon other creatures of the earth as objects to exploit for our own purposes, invading their necessary habitats to the unprecedented point that the extinction of several entire species occurs daily.[11] Is it surprising in all the getting and spending, that we tend also to treat other people as objects to manipulate and exploit? Even the sacredness of human life and relationships has been submerged under the weight of commercial interaction.

Some argue that the Judeo-Christian tradition itself, which charges human beings to "have dominion over" the creatures and to "subdue" the earth (Gen. 1:28), is responsible for Western culture's ecological destructiveness. It is not the charge of scripture itself but the self-interested interpretation of those words that has proved so harmful. Why should the dominance that humans seem to have by virtue of self-reflective, conscious intelligence be an excuse for brutal and destructive domination? Surely the rule of the human being over the earth was intended to reflect the rule of God over creation—an authority marked by loving care, creativity, responsible stewardship, and joy in the beauty and power of life itself.

We have much to unlearn from our Western heritage. In this task we would benefit by opening our hearts to the wisdom of societies we often have disdained as "primitive," including that of our Native American citizens. I also find it significant that within the Christian heritage, the churches of the Orthodox East have expressed the greatest reverence for the earth. In Orthodox theology, the material of creation is given to us as a vehicle of God's grace so that all life is a sacrament. What we need are the eyes to see material life for what it is—the Spirit-bearing means of a loving relationship with God and with one another. Today more than ever, the church universal needs to recover the sacramentality of the created order. We would do well to listen carefully to the theology of our Eastern Christian friends.

If human consciousness is to preserve the holiness that the entire creation radiates, it will take great vigilance on the part of all individuals and communities worldwide who share the vision. In our culture, that will entail special responsibility for those private institutions carrying our traditions of faith. Through her members, the church has a vital role to play in fostering an awareness of the sacredness of life and in modeling an appropriate response to that awareness. Families of faith can become bearers of the new consciousness that will be required for this indispensable task. We will consider specific ways in which the family can respond to our current ecological crisis in chapters 4 and 8.

In sum, the forms of darkness in our world can feel overwhelming to an institution as small and seemingly fragile as the family. Indeed, the destructive elements of our culture have had an enormous impact on the health and stability of family life. In countless ways, they also have diminished the church's faithful witness to the new creation in Christ. Too often, the church has been little more than a sad reflection of the distorted values and ambitions of the society it serves. Human sin is abundantly evident in the church on earth. Yet the promise of new life—an unyielding alternative to the values and behaviors of the world—lies at the very heart of the church's identity and the identity of each constituent member. Because families are, by nature, intensive laboratories of human relationship, families within the church are, by vocation, key players in the drama of transformation that marks the hope and promise of Christian faith.

## *For Reflection*

～What forms of darkness in our society are particularly disturbing to you?

～Which of these do you experience as having the most destructive impact on family life in general? on your family in particular?

～How might your answers change if your family lived in different socioeconomic conditions?

# 4

# Becoming Sacred Shelters

~

*It will not do to heap his grave with flowers.*
*Flowers wilt and die.*
*Rather let us shelter him as he has sheltered us—*
*Gather words— soft-spoken, deliberate,*
*    love-tipped,*
*Deep rooted thoughts, nursed with tolerance.*
*More vital even than the cinder-block and wood,*
*These walls he built have made the world home for us.*
*And this great gift remains good:*
*Because he was, we are ourselves.*

— Mary Hynes-Berry
for Emerson Hynes 1915–71

A HEALTHY FAMILY IS A SHELTER whose walls can offer needed protection from the more injurious values of the culture. Yet the protective embrace of the family needs to become an increasingly permeable membrane through which larger realities are mediated, so that gradually we come to know where we stand in a world filled with darkness, light, and ambiguity.

Dolores Leckey calls the Christian family a "sacred shelter,"[1] by which she means "a place of acceptance, nurture, and growth that empowers family members to participate . . . in

God's ongoing acts of compassion and salvation."[2] The family of faith cannot protect its members fully from the pain and brokenness of the world, but it can offer a context for understanding and engaging life in the world from a place of stability and love. Like the larger church of which it is a particular expression, such a family can provide a framework of faith and offer healing for life's wounds, reconciliation for breached relationships, and support for the mission of each family member.

Leckey makes it clear that the phrase "sacred shelter" in no way implies family narcissism or isolation from the needs and concerns of society as a whole. "On the contrary," she emphasizes, "it releases its members for the pastoral care of the world."[3] The "pastoral care of the world" is one way of interpreting the task of the church in which member families may participate. Yet to be prepared and freed for such a task, the family must learn to offer its own members adequate pastoral care.

How do families become sacred shelters in which consistent nurturing and the keeping of a common faith issue in creative ministry to the world? In the introduction, I indicated that part of our task would be "to discover the spiritual disciplines inherent in the very structure and nature of family life" and that part would be "to explore creative ways to incorporate time-honored practices into contemporary family life." Although it is difficult to separate the two elements of this task categorically, the current chapter represents a direct focus on the first. The second part of our task will require several chapters as we consider specific practices of prayer, scriptural reflection, celebrative ritual, and service in relation to busy families today.

## Reflecting God's Love

In this chapter we will examine an expression of spiritual formation that is intrinsically suited to family life because of its intensive relational structure. Family life is structured to provide physical, emotional, mental, and spiritual nurture to its members. As we underscored at the beginning, *relationships*—their character, quality, and purpose—are absolutely central to the very nature of the family. From the standpoint of faith, we have said that the way we relate to one another must be identified as *the* quintessential spiritual discipline of family life.

As people who are joined to the body of Christ, we are called to an expression of domestic life that reflects God's love, just as we are called to reflect that love in the whole of our lives. Some of the ways in which families have natural opportunities to reflect God's love are through presence, acceptance, affirmation, accountability, forgiveness, and hospitality.

## *Presence*

Perhaps the most foundational expression of spiritual grace within the home is the quality of our presence to one another. Author Wendy Wright states simply, "God is present when we are present to one another. . . . God wears the faces of those whose lives we share."[4] Yet we all know how hard it is truly to be present to one another. Often we find ourselves distracted or preoccupied by tasks, problems, feelings, and fantasies. We are, as someone once aptly said to me, "rehashing the past or rehearsing the future." It takes effort and intention to focus on the presence of another person, as well as a willingness to give oneself over to the need of the other at a given time. Such presence is the root of authentic listening, and listening is the foundation of real communication and communion among persons.

Naturally at times we are more or less capable of being present to one another. Each family will have its own patterns. Many parents identify bedtime rituals as the time of day they are most able to be fully present to their children. Some find that the evening meal affords the best occasion. One single mother told me that about the only time she had during the work week with her kids was in the station wagon, driving them to school. She turned off the radio and listened with full attention to her children during that daily drive.

Even households disrupted by severe dysfunction can experience precious moments of genuine presence. One woman's experience of family life was so "scarred by drug-dependency, verbal and physical abuse, and alcoholism" that she could scarcely put the words *God* and *family* together. But when invited to reflect on any regular occasions when she and her children experienced one another's presence, she realized that such a time existed: "It was at the kitchen sink while washing dishes."[5] Somehow, when two people were standing side by side engaged in this common daily task, they could begin to speak to each other with civility and care. No one ever intruded on this time. It seemed tacitly understood by the family as sacred, inviolable space. Her story is important because it reveals that the possibility of presence to one another can be realized under the most difficult and painful of family circumstances.

### *Acceptance*

A grace closely related to the gift of presence is acceptance. By this I mean a complete and unconditional acceptance of each person as a precious and beloved child of God. This attitude is a reflection of God's unconditional love for us. It is altogether possible for us to accept people without accepting their behaviors or actions. Indeed, the distinction between our essential being and our particular attitudes or conduct seems imperative to me, yet it is not one we make easily. How often parents say, "You are a bad boy" or "You are a good girl," when what they mean is that the child's behavior is good or bad. We tend to equate a child's identity with conduct, when we could be more accurate with our language: "What you *did* was unacceptable and has consequences, but I know you are capable of making better choices."

A mother once told me how this dynamic was played out in her family. Her husband, exasperated by some foolish thing their five-year old son had done, yelled at the boy telling him how stupid he was. The little boy looked shocked and puzzled. Then he said, "Daddy, I know what I *did* was really dumb, but *I* am not stupid." His father, realizing immediately how inaccurate and needlessly damaging his words had been, apologized to his son.

It is a spiritual discipline of the highest order to accept family members as worthy of our continued love when they choose ideals, values, or beliefs in sharp contrast to our own. If we are not well grounded in the truth of God's unconditional love for us, it is difficult to offer such love to others.

To love in God's way involves generous self-giving. A vital family life requires a great deal of give and take—the capacity for compromise, yielding to others, and graciously being yielded to. We will find it hard to give ourselves freely to others when we are judging them. I speak of judgment here in the sense of condemnation rather than of discernment. The condemning face of judgment is a form of withholding personal acceptance, thus a way of withholding the self.

Unconditional acceptance becomes the basis for genuine mutual commitment. The strength of commitment and support between spouses is the foundation of a secure and healthy family life. Spouses who become parents are the backbone of the complex nexus of relationships we call family; they are its means of financial support as well as emotional, educational, and spiritual support. The quality of a husband and wife's mutuality becomes a significant model for growing children. If parents desire children to develop healthy and committed relationships with their siblings and friends, they will want to recognize the impact of the modeling provided in their own relationship as spouses.

Single parents feel the weight of trying to model alone. In these circumstances, it is often helpful to draw adult friends, godparents, grandparents, or other relatives into family life with greater frequency. The modeling of relationships between caring adults is vital. Yet parents also provide meaningful models in the way they relate to their children, a dynamic with particular significance in single-parent families.

## Affirmation

Acceptance of each person as a beloved child of God is the ground for authentic affirmation. By affirmation I mean the capacity to recognize and encourage the unique gifts and personality of each family member. Spouses who were attracted to each other by common interests and shared values often find it hard to accept significant differences that may emerge as intimacy grows over the course of a marriage. Parents are frequently astonished by how different their children can be from one another, not to mention from their parents. It can be a rather rude shock just how much variety issues from a common gene-pool!

Years ago I was given a book in which the authors contrasted "architect parents" and "farmer parents." As you might imagine, architect parents have a blueprint in mind for their child. They have often decided (sometimes quite unconsciously) what talents they will encourage and what traits they will not tolerate. The child is expected to follow the parents' expectations for achievement, career, and sometimes even marriage. Farmer parents, on the other hand, know that their children, like different plants, have different requirements for growth. Just as certain plants require more sun or water than others, some children need more structure or encouragement than others. Farmer parents observe their children's personality traits and talents and learn ways of nurturing each accordingly.[6]

When parents can recognize and affirm their children's genuine gifts, they set their children free for joyful growth. Inability or unwillingness to accept a child's natural talents stifles growth and generates anxiety in the child. Yet when we cherish classical music and our kid is a natural rock drummer; when we love sports and our child prefers to bury her nose in a book; when we value community service and our children make a beeline for a career in the stock market—it takes great inner freedom to affirm their distinctive gifts and personalities!

Family members need to encourage the goodness and giftedness they see in one another. Given the highly competitive and critical tenor of our culture, it will take intentional effort on the part of families to make the home a different kind of environment—one in which cooperation seems more natural than competition and competition is engaged in with a light touch, for fun. Naturally, a child needs to feel secure and worthwhile in order to offer praise or encouragement to another child. But if that child has been nurtured in a loving and trustworthy environment, the generous impulse can be fostered as well. Children need to be taught that to affirm another child's talent or character does not deny or subtract from their own gifts. Adult modeling, both with other adults and with children, is essential here. Moreover, our understanding of the body of Christ, with all

its necessary and different members, could be fruitfully empha-
sized within the home to counteract the individualism and com-
petitiveness of our society.

## *Accountability*

It goes without saying that some attitudes and forms of conduct
cannot and should not be affirmed. We know too much these
days about choices that are clearly dysfunctional, both in the
lives of those who make them and those they affect. Substance
abuse, physical, emotional, and sexual abuse, infidelity, and a
wide range of other compulsive, irresponsible behaviors call for
what is often termed "tough love." This is love that cares enough
about persons to confront them when their attitudes and conduct
have become destructive. It is the kind of love that challenges us
to stand accountable for how our choices affect ourselves, our
families, and our wider communities.

When we stand firmly on the ground of unconditional
acceptance of one another as beloved children of God and are
prepared to affirm and encourage one another's genuine gifts, we
are also in a good position to confront one another with needed
challenges from a posture of love. The apostle Paul calls this
spiritual art "speaking the truth in love" (Ephesians 4:15). It is
truly a demanding skill, beginning with the discipline of
discerning what is true and following with the capacity both to
offer authentic appreciation when fitting and to confront gently
yet firmly when needed. Loving challenge requires unblinking
honesty and heartfelt compassion. The deceptively simple
phrase, "speaking the truth in love," clearly indicates that *the
spirit in which one speaks truth is as important as the truth one
speaks.*

Jesus' ministry gave ample evidence of a love that called
people to account for their attitudes and conduct. He was not
afraid to confront those who imagined that their true motives
were hidden and that their outward behavior was beyond
reproach. Nor did he shy away from telling someone who needed
to hear it, "go and sin no more." Authentic Christian love does
not capitulate to sin. It does not condone or enable life-
destroying patterns. In the language of the contemporary

recovery movement, genuine love is not "codependent." Love desires nothing less for the beloved than complete well-being, the promise of abundant life in Christ. Such well-being is possible only if we are willing to hold one another responsible for our choices and actions in relationship.

Accountability is another way to speak about justice. Biblically speaking, justice means right relationship with fellow human beings. God's call to deal rightly with one another is never absent from our lives, and at times we are obliged to remind one another of this persistent call. Yet none of us measures up to God's standards of justice. Not one of us treats everyone rightly all the time. That is why forgiveness is so critical to the health of human community.

### *Forgiveness*

Forgiveness is the thorniest of bushes with the most splendid of roses. Nothing goes to the heart of the relational spirituality of family life more than the dynamics of forgiveness and reconciliation. And nothing so profoundly expresses the core of the Christian spiritual life. At the center of Christian faith stands the cross, representing God's forgiveness of and reconciliation with us. This *undeserved* act of mercy and love is the soil from which we are called to forgive one another.

Yet we have much difficulty with forgiveness. That difficulty stems from the emotional side of human life. When we have been deeply wounded by another person or group, it can *feel* impossible to forgive. In truth, we cannot force ourselves to forgive against our will, for it would not then be real.

We do sometimes try to *make* ourselves forgive out of a sense of Christian duty. When we do so, I think we are prone to a number of traps. For example, we put the offender on probation,[7] waiting impatiently for evidence that the person deserves the gift we imagine we have so graciously bestowed. When such evidence is not forthcoming, we suddenly withdraw the "gift." Sometimes we try to deny that we were really hurt after all or to take inappropriate blame for being hurt, so that there is no longer any offense to forgive. Another trap is to engage in that "martyr complex" where we rather enjoy the distinction of being offended and gain satisfaction in "forgiving" the other with all the fanfare and display of the self-consciously wronged person.

I do not believe that forgiveness is to be equated with excusing a person's offensive attitudes or destructive behaviors. Certain *conduct* should never be excused, even though the *person* who chooses to engage in it can be forgiven. Neither do I subscribe to the notion that forgiving necessarily means forgetting. Perhaps for small pricks and indignities we can excuse and forget. But for major assaults that leave us gasping with psychic pain, we will find ourselves incapable of either.

Forgiveness is more profound and more costly than any of these substitutes. It is really only possible through the power of the divine Spirit. Blessedly, we are assured that what is impossible for human beings is possible with God. As Lewis Smedes puts it, "Forgiveness seems almost unnatural. Our sense of fairness tells us people should pay for the wrong they do. But forgiving is love's power to break nature's rule."[8] Our forgiveness then is a participation in the gracious mercy of God.

To forgive is to make a conscious choice to release the person who has wounded us from the sentence of our judgment, however just or fair the judgment. It is an active decision to call forth and rebuild the love that grounds our relationship and, in so doing, to leave behind our resentment and desire for retribution. Of course it helps enormously if the offender is willing to admit guilt and ask for forgiveness, but we may not make remorse a condition for the forgiveness that reflects God's love. It is possible to forgive others from the heart without their ever seeking or receiving it consciously.

We have a vivid contemporary example of such unilateral forgiveness in Beulah Mae Donald, a black woman whose teenage son was brutally lynched by a group of Alabama Klansmen not so many years ago. At the end of a trial that brought to light all the sordid details of hate-inspired violence, one of the convicted Klansmen turned to the mother of the slain boy and in a voice shaking with emotion asked if she could ever forgive him. Mrs. Donald, who had quietly wept through the trial, looked straight at him and said, "I do forgive you. From the day I found out who you all was, I asked God to take care of y'all, and He has."[9]

Beulah Mae Donald's forgiveness was just as real before it was asked for as after. Her capacity to forgive did not depend on the contrition of her son's slayer. But the full potential of her forgiveness was not realized until the Klansman asked for and received it. The promise of reconciliation at the heart of forgiveness cannot be fulfilled until it is received and acknowledged. It always takes two parties to bring the gift of forgiveness to fruition in renewed relationship.

However, we need to acknowledge that not all of us are capable of responding to traumatic injustice the way Mrs. Donald did. Some of us are more mature in our sense of personhood and in our faith than others. It may require significant emotional healing in the person who has been victimized before forgiveness becomes a real possibility. In some circumstances, forgiveness can be offered prematurely—either for the victim or perpetrator. Many have been helped by understanding forgiveness as a process. Coming to a point in our spiritual journey where we *desire* to forgive our offender can take time.

Yet a time may come when we simply tire of living with the constant shadow of bitterness that saps our energy and eats away our peace of heart. Forgiveness frees the forgiver as well as the forgiven. Resentment is a burden well shed. A time may come when we begin to see in ourselves weaknesses not unlike those of the person who wounded us, and we gain both a sense of personal humility and compassion for the offender. A time may come when the resistance of our heart to another person melts away suddenly and surprisingly because a whole new picture of the situation that caused our hurt has emerged. There is so much we do not see and cannot know about those who wound us. Perhaps that is why we are counseled to leave judgment to God, the searcher of all hearts.

In light of the profundity and difficulty of forgiveness, it is instructive to observe that children often forgive much more readily and naturally than adults. Ernest Boyer tells a story from his family that may bring a smile of recognition to many parents.

The older son was about to go out and buy a Christmas present for his younger brother when he discovered that the same brother had just broken one of his favorite toys. Outraged, the older boy loudly proclaimed he wouldn't get a Christmas gift for his little brother after all. A moment later he was putting his coat on, announcing to Mom that he was going. Where? To buy the present, of course. The response to his mother's unconcealed surprise was simply, "Well, he *is* my brother, isn't he?"[10] Boyer reminds us that children live much more in the present than do adults, which often allows them to release the past quickly and to refocus on relationships moment by moment.

A family that practices the art of forgiveness knows increasing joy and freedom in their relationships. Forgiveness and reconciliation are preeminent signs of the vitality of God's spirit within the crucible of intimacy that constitutes family life.

## *Hospitality*

Finally, the family is the most natural place to practice hospitality to friends and strangers. Because family is the place of our most intimate relationships, the meaning of true hospitality is best expressed by bringing those outside the circle of intimacy into its very center. Sharing the bounty not only of food but of loving care, personal presence, and joyful living is ministry indeed. "Everything that goes into making a home flows out of those who enter," says Leckey.[11] There is an ancient practice in the church of welcoming all guests into one's home as one would welcome Christ himself. The beauty of such hospitality is that its blessing is mutual:

> An ancient Irish rune tells of a stranger passed on the road. Food and drink were made ready, and there was welcome in the heart should the stranger stop at the croft. He did, and all were blessed; not only those who served and spoke with him, but the cattle and the small children at their play, and the old folk who sat nodding by the fire. "And the lark said in her song, 'Often, often, often goes the Christ in the stranger's guise.'"[12]

The practice of hospitality reminds us that the family of faith does not exist for its own sake but is connected intrinsically to a wider world.

## Supporting the Child's Religious Experience

In a family that is conscious of being or becoming a sacred shelter, there is an important place for giving support to the child's inborn spiritual experience. Indeed, this aspect of adult nurture for children is a core expression of acceptance, affirmation, and hospitality within the home.

Although we have been looking primarily at the role adults play in reflecting God's love to their children, many parents have the uncanny sense that their children reflect God's love just as clearly (or more clearly!) to them. The capacity to release hurts, forgive, and pick up again in the present moment is but one of many ways in which children unconsciously become guides to adults in the spiritual life.

Children have an innate capacity to relate to God, a truth that often amazes and unnerves adults. Yet it should not surprise us. Someone once said to me, "You realize, don't you, that children have come from God more recently than we?" Perceiving children's spiritual capacity is nothing new. An old Italian adage declares, "God and the child speak the same language."[13]

Sofia Cavalletti, a pioneer in the arena of children's spirituality, has garnered some profound insights from her years of observing and working with young children:

> We believe that the child, more than any other, has need of love because the child . . . is rich in love. The child's need to be loved depends not so much on a lack that requires filling, but on a richness that seeks something that corresponds to it. . . . The child needs an infinite, global love, such as no human being is able to give . . . in the contact with God the child finds the nourishment his [or her] being requires. . . . God—who is Love—and the child, who asks for love more than [for] mother's milk, thus meet one another in a particular correspondence of nature. . . . In helping the child's religious life, far from imposing

something that is foreign . . . , we are responding to the child's silent request: "Help me to come closer to God by myself."[14]

Cavalletti's writings are full of stories that reveal sometimes astonishing perceptions on the part of children—perceptions surpassing what they've been taught. She tells, for example, of a three-year-old girl raised in an atheistic family with neither nursery school nor church contact, who asked her father, "Where did the world come from?" After explaining his understanding of the world's origins in a scientific framework, her father acknowledged, "However, there are those who say that all this comes from a very powerful being, and they call him God." At this, the little girl began whirling around the room in joy, exclaiming with great excitement, "I knew what you told me wasn't true; it is Him, it is Him!"[15]

Perhaps more remarkable is the story of young Irina, a Soviet girl of atheistic parents who visited her adult cousin and saw an icon of Jesus for the first time. As her cousin tried awkwardly to explain the meaning of the icon, Irina said, "You know, I knew He existed and I have always talked with Him before going to sleep; I knew He was everywhere and that He sees me when I get into mischief, only sometimes I was afraid of Him. How can I speak with Him?" The child desired to kiss the icon but not in the way she would kiss her mother, "Because He is greater than my mother . . . He is better than everyone, and He loves me." When the girl's mother arrived, she cried out, "Mommy . . . He loves you too. At last I've seen His face, but I've known Him for a long time." Her embarrassed mother took the icon away from Irina, who wept, repeating over and over, "I want to see Him, I need to talk to Him."[16]

I share these stories here to illustrate a critical point: Children often have their own experiences of God unbidden, and they certainly have the capacity to relate to God in their own way. Our task as faithful parents and educators is to support and encourage children's innate religious sensibilities, not to "give" them a capacity they may well have in greater abundance than we. No one can *give* another person faith. Faith is a gift only God can draw from the human heart. We merely affirm, support, and encourage faith in one another at whatever stage of growth it is expressed. Adults can communicate the depth, conviction, and passion of their own faith to children; but they cannot thereby ensure that their children will accept those convictions. Children must find faith for themselves, a simple truth expressed in the phrase "God has no grandchildren." Cavalletti's catechetical approach with young children is instructive in this regard, and Carol Dittberner expresses it beautifully:

> We do not try to stand between God and the child and impart answers or information. We listen with the children and together we ask, "God, who are you? How do you love us?" Together we meditate on the questions and the answers in the scripture. . . . What we hope to create is the opportunity for the child's development through religious experience rather than through lessons."[17]

Children can surprise us with the immediacy of their spiritual perceptions. What they need most from adults are the affirmation and support of those perceptions, the context of religious tradition by which to understand their own experience, and a language with which to express their faith. That is the import of little Irina's question, "How can I speak with Him?" Cavalletti's catechesis offers young children simple but beautiful words for prayer like *alleluia, hosanna, rejoice, praise God, shalom,* and *amen.* Joy is the primary hallmark of the young child's experience of God; the prayer of children under age six is that of praise, thanks, and blessing. It is only later that children begin praying petition and intercession naturally.

The language of faith we offer children needs to include movement, signs, and acts as well as words. Young children need concrete forms of expression. Gestures such as kneeling, bowing, passing the peace, making the sign of the cross, lifting hands in praise or folding them in prayer can be helpful. Children need active movement as much in their spiritual as in their physical development. They also need tangible, visible signs and symbols in order to assimilate the message of faith. That would seem to be the import of Irina's desire to see the icon of Jesus and to touch it with a kiss of veneration. She felt that seeing his image would help her "talk with Him."

Such considerations bring us to the simple but specific practices suggested in the next several chapters. Families may become sacred shelters in many ways. Within the framework of healthy relationships that reflect and embody God's love, we can now explore ways of incorporating prayer, Bible stories, special celebrations, and expressions of service into family life.

## *For Reflection*

∽How have you experienced God's love reflected in your family?

∽When do you find you can be most fully present to your family members?

∽Did you experience genuine acceptance and affirmation as a child, and if so, from whom? How do you express acceptance and affirmation in your family life now?

∽Can you describe authentic experiences of "tough love" and forgivness in your life? What do you yearn for with respect to these practices?

∽Are you familiar with instances of a child's innate relationship with God? How do you think families can best support the natural bond between God and the child?

# 5

# Prayer in the Family

⌇

*And in the morning, a great while before day, he rose and*
*went out to a lonely place, and there he prayed.*
—Mark 1:35, RSV

PRAYER IS ABSOLUTELY CENTRAL and indispensable to
the spiritual life. That is why the Gospels show us
Jesus rising long before dawn to go off to a lonely
place to pray. It is why Paul urges, "Pray without
ceasing" (1 Thess. 5:17, KJV). It is why the Eastern churches still
adhere to the fourth-century declaration of Evagrius Ponticus:
"A theologian is one whose prayer is true."[1] It is why no less a
scholar than John Calvin, better known for his doctrine of
predestination than of prayer, exalts prayer as "the chief exercise
of faith." Indeed, he proclaims with simple directness, "Words
fail to explain how necessary prayer is."[2]

What is in the nature of prayer that makes it the life breath
of a vital faith? What possesses someone like John Wesley to
declare, "God does nothing but in answer to prayer"?[3] The only
adequate response is that prayer is the very heart of our encounter and relationship with God. Without prayer, there is no mutual
relationship, no communication, no growth. Prayer is the inward
expression of our faith; it is the means of communion with our
Maker, a means God graciously gives us through the Holy Spirit.
Like all spiritual disciplines, it is first a gift, but a gift we appropriate through effort.

If prayer constitutes the soul of the Christian spiritual life,
prayer also must lie at the center of family spirituality. Martin

73

Luther, who was nothing if not a family man, once declared, "I have so much business I cannot get on without spending three hours daily in prayer."[4] While such a statement seems overwhelming in one sense, it is profoundly encouraging in another: Evidently family life and serious prayer are not mutually exclusive!

The conscious, daily, personal prayer of each family member is essential to a spiritually whole family life because it roots our relationships with others in the ground of our relationship with God. Out of that deeper ground, we find ourselves growing more according to God's design than our own. Authentic prayer, of necessity, changes us; there is simply no possibility of encountering the living God without being changed. Prayer demands that we acknowledge our limits and invite God's grace. It reveals us to ourselves in our truest colors, meticulously sifting out the judging, clinging, controlling sides of the personality from gifts of patience, charity, and courage.

When we are engaged in the genuine exercise of prayer and not merely in efforts to impose our agenda on God, we discover very quickly that God will not be manipulated in prayer. For example, we cannot pray truly for our children without recognizing that each child, given into our care for so short a time, has a unique human autonomy that ultimately belongs to God alone. Nor can we pray for our spouses without encountering the same inviolable mystery of personhood.

Many problems in marriage seem to derive from one of two delusions: (1) I find myself primarily in my spouse (I become a reflection of my spouse's image—a delusion to which many women have been susceptible); or (2) I find my spouse primarily in myself (my spouse becomes a reflection of my image—a delusion to which many men have been prone). The same delusional dynamics have wreaked havoc on many parent-child relationships. Sometimes mothers have tried to find their sense of worth through their children, and fathers have manipulated children into living out their own unfulfilled dreams. But God does not want us to attempt to make anyone else in our image or to give over our identity to anyone except God, in whom our true being is confirmed and fulfilled.

Prayer is the altar on which our illusions are immolated, because in prayer we face the one relationship that is the source of truth about all other relationships: Each of us has his or her being in God alone. If we seek life elsewhere for ourselves or others, our expectations will be defeated.

## The Bonding of Prayer

That common phrase, "The family that prays together stays together," doubtless strikes sophisticated ears as trite. Yet a truth resides beneath the glib exterior. There is a bonding power in prayer that goes deeper than the best interpersonal communication skills. Prayer is not a substitute for good communication, but it plumbs a depth of reality unavailable at the purely "horizontal" level. Prayer draws the mystery of God into what we would otherwise perceive as strictly human interaction. When I hear my husband pray for me, I see my relationship with him in a new light, one mediated by the grace of Christ. Hearing family members praying with sincerity for one another can forge deep connections.

Of course, prayer need not be heard to have an impact on shaping the quality and character of our relationships. Simply knowing that a person is praying for you can alter your sense of relationship with that person, and the reality of another person's prayer can at times be felt as a palpable support.

Most of us are completely unconscious of being prayed for, yet even here we may sense a particular quality of care and connection with the person who is praying for us without our knowledge. Secret prayer can have remarkable results, not the least of which is the spiritual bond it creates whether or not we are aware of it. Richard Foster describes one of the ways he enjoys praying for his children at night when they are asleep: Laying hands lightly on them, he imagines the light of Christ healing any trauma from the day and filling them with peace.[5] Foster acknowledges the receptivity of sleeping people to the influence of prayer. At that time, conscious barriers to God's grace are relaxed. Here is one simple yet profound way for parents to form deeper bonds with their children in and through the all-encompassing bond of God's love.

## Ways of Prayer

Prayer needs to be modeled and taught in very simple ways in the home. Since we are spiritual beings at root, prayer can become as native to us as breathing. One particularly natural form is conversational prayer. Christians and Jews believe in a personal God with whom human beings can have a personal relationship. Christians also believe that God has come to us "in person" through Jesus whom we call the Christ. Therefore, we can speak to God or Christ just as we would speak with another person. The difference is that this Person is worthy not only of our greatest possible love and respect but also of our worship. As the One who creates, redeems, and sustains us, God knows and loves us more deeply than any other person can.

Children who are at ease talking are usually comfortable with conversational prayer. It is helpful to both children and adults to realize that no special words or particular phrases are necessary; praying this way is simply a matter of communicating to God what is in the heart. Sometimes it is useful for parents to help children articulate their thoughts and feelings first to other family members. It then becomes a simple step to turn these same thoughts and feelings into the words with which children address God.

Conversational prayer, although doubtless most common, is simply one form among many. As noted earlier, young children naturally tend to offer thanks and praise. Single words or short phrases can express their joy in God: *holy, thank you, bless the Lord.* Teaching children some of the less familiar biblical words for prayer, such as *alleluia* and *shalom*, can give them a richer language to express the wonder and mystery of life. Because many older children and even adults have difficulty praying aloud in a group, the use of single words or brief phrases often proves an enormously freeing way to pray.

## The Place of the Body in Prayer

Beyond words, the language of prayer becomes boundless. We have discussed the importance of offering children some symbolic gestures for prayer, such as bowing, kneeling, folding the hands or raising them. While no particular gesture is necessary for God to hear us, many forms of movement might express what is deepest in our hearts. Running, jumping, shouting, or dancing might best convey the exuberance of a child's joy; curling up in a ball or resting one's head in cupped hands might express one child's sadness, while the same gesture might signify peace and contentedness for another child. Children have their own nonverbal language for prayer, which can be encouraged along with verbal prayer forms.

Grown-ups have the same capacity, but it is often more deeply buried and difficult to recover. Most adults have grown extremely self-conscious about movement in worship, being unaccustomed to using the body in prayer and fearful of appearing awkward. Some also fear that particular gestures may identify them with a group whose theology or practice discomforts them. Thus they exclude some of the simplest and most natural movements (such as the raising of hands) and some of the most ancient gestures (such as signing the cross) from the realm of possibility.

One of the beauties of family worship, especially with young children, is the freedom it affords to experiment with bodily participation in prayer. Within the accepting circle of family love, in the relative privacy and informality of family worship, perhaps adults can learn to express their feelings more naturally in prayer, allowing their bodies to help rather than hinder that expression. It might mean something as simple as holding hands, linking arms, or raising one's palms upward in a gesture of receptivity during intercessory prayers. It might mean kneeling together for confession or discovering a unique family gesture for blessing one another. At first, expect that such movement will feel a bit artificial and awkward. But with time and use, the gestures that seem authentic will emerge. No one should be forced in any respect, however. Only as we experience movement's enhancing our worship will we find it freeing.

## The Place of Imagination in Prayer

Another form of prayer that seems particularly well suited to younger children is imaginative prayer. Richard Foster provides a lovely example through an incident where he was called to the home of a seriously ill baby. The infant had a four-year-old brother. Foster, aware that "children can often pray with unusual effectiveness," enlisted the child's help in praying for his little sister:

> "Let's play a little game," I said. "Since we know that Jesus is always with us, let's imagine that he is sitting over in the chair across from us. He is waiting patiently for us to center our attention on him. When we see him, we start thinking more about his love than how sick Julie is. He smiles, gets up, and comes over to us. Then let's both put our hands on Julie, and when we do, Jesus will put his hands on top of ours. We'll watch the light from Jesus flow right into your little sister and make her well. Let's watch the healing power of Christ fight with the bad germs until they are all gone. Okay!" Seriously the little one nodded. Together we prayed in this childlike way and then thanked the Lord that what we had prayed was the way it was going to be. . . . The next morning Julie was perfectly well.[6]

Foster's way of praying with the child is presented as a form of play—a "game" that uses the child's natural capacity for imagination and trust. Yet like all child's play, it is serious business with real consequences. Here again, as adults and parents we can learn much from children if we are willing to encourage and facilitate their innate abilities.

Visualization for healing has broad application. Much has been written on the effective use of visualization by children with serious diseases such as cancer. Sometimes we forget that smaller arenas of life's hurts call for the attention of prayer too. I know parents who have taught their children to place their hands over a simple bruise or cut, close their eyes, and imagine Jesus' healing light flowing through their hands.

Families can learn to use imagination in their intercessory prayer. Here is one possible process: First, all are asked to visualize the person in need enfolded by God's light and warmth; then they are invited to "see" the light gently penetrating any darkness or pain, gradually making the person whole. A variety of images for the healing process may be suggested: ice melting or confusion being ordered. The advantage of imaginative prayer is that it does not depend on our capacity to verbalize. This enables greater participation by young children and often is experienced as a deeply moving and refreshing alternative for adults as well.

One aspect of imaginative intercession that should not be neglected is releasing the person prayed for into God's healing hands at the end of the prayer. After lifting up persons in need, we leave them with God until we are consciously ready to remember them in prayer again. This involves recognition that God is continually working grace in the lives of those we pray for, which releases us from the imagined burden of carrying them by ourselves.

Some people of faith believe the best response to crisis in a loved one's life is the practice of "releasing prayer." We do what we reasonably can from a physical, emotional, or spiritual standpoint, depending on the nature of the crisis. But beyond such responses, and particularly in situations where the problem seems chronic or intractable, there is the more difficult task of letting go our desire for control over the outcome. It is a real discipline to entrust our loved ones to God's care, releasing them from our often overly anxious concern and sometimes interfering ways of caring. With the grace to let go and trust God comes the gift of freedom. Releasing prayer is nonmanipulative, giving expression to the freedom and trust that are signs of mature love. Perhaps it is in this sense that T. S. Eliot writes his celebrated poetic phrase, "Teach us to care and not to care."[7]

## The Practice of Breath Prayers

Yet another simple form of prayer well suited to family life is what author Ron DelBene calls "breath prayer."[8] This is a contemporary adaptation of one of the most ancient and time-honored forms of prayer. It consists of the repetition of a short prayer phrase. In biblical times, devout Jews meditated on a brief portion of a psalm or other scripture by saying it aloud softly, repeating it over and over until it became one with the soul and could be lived by heart. Early on, Christians developed similar forms of prayer, the best known of which is called "The Jesus Prayer." In essence, it combines the prayer of the publican in Luke 18:13, "God, be merciful to me, a sinner!" and the earliest creed of the church, "Jesus is Lord." The full form is, "Lord Jesus Christ, son of the living God, have mercy on me, a sinner."

DelBene suggests that we each find our own prayer, the prayer of our heart. We do that by asking two questions: "What is my name for God?" and "What is my deep desire?" If we can answer these and put them together in a brief phrase, we have our breath prayer. The address for God should be familiar and authentic; the desire ought to be the deepest and most encompassing within our awareness. The phrase needs to be short and simple enough to say in a breath; it will alter naturally if the rhythm is not comfortable for repetition. Below are some sample breath prayers:

> "Lord, show me your love."
> "Jesus, teach me humility."
> "Let me trust you, O God."

Saint Francis had such a prayer—"My God and my All!"—that he repeated over and over during private prayer watches at night.

Many Christians use a brief scriptural phrase in much the same way. A passage such as "Be still and know that I am God," "The Lord is my shepherd," "Perfect love casts out fear," or "Worship the Lord in the beauty of holiness," can function in much the same way as a breath prayer. Sometimes a tune or a hymn stanza can carry this kind of prayer for us.

Once we have found our prayer, we can take it with us throughout the day. We can use it in all kinds of situations that might otherwise be considered wasted time—waiting in lines, traffic jams, or airports. It can also make a joy of routine activities such as household chores that engage only the surface mind. Breath prayers are excellent companions for walking, jogging, swimming, and long-distance driving. Once the prayer has lodged in the subconscious mind, we will find it surfacing of its own accord at various points in the day.

Breath prayers are useful for children because they are so simple and because children tend to respond positively to the stability of repetition. Everyone in a family who so chooses can have a breath prayer, which may change over the years as the individual grows and prayers are either fulfilled or transformed. There are seasons, however, especially during crises, when family members may wish to pray one member's breath prayer with that person as a way of entering into the need supportively. In his book *Into the Light*, DelBene describes how breath prayer can be used among families and caregivers for people who are seriously ill or who are facing death.[9] I find it particularly moving and useful material.

## Nurturing a
## Contemplative Attitude in the Home

One of the most profound effects of a simple tool like the breath prayer is that it gradually makes us more aware of God's presence in the midst of everyday activities. All regular spiritual disciplines have the ultimate effect of honing our faculties of attentiveness to God's loving presence. As we become more attuned to the divine reality that underlies daily life, we can begin to live even the smallest things prayerfully. Particular practices of prayer foster a capacity for contemplative living in us. Thomas Kelly, the great Quaker teacher and writer, gives voice to this experience in his beloved classic, *A Testament of Devotion*:

> There is a way of ordering our mental life on more than one level at once. On one level we may be thinking, discussing, seeing, calculating, meeting all the demands of external affairs. But deep within, behind the scenes, at a profounder level, we may also be in prayer and adoration, song and worship and a gentle receptiveness to divine breathings.[10]

Kelly's words bring to mind those of a seventeenth-century Carmelite monk known as Brother Lawrence, who spoke of "practicing the presence of God" through "a silent, secret and nearly unbroken conversation of the soul with God." The early prayer disciplines of his life brought Brother Lawrence to the point where he could honestly say, "The time of business is no different from the time of prayer. In the noise and clatter of my kitchen, I possess God as tranquilly as if I were upon my knees before the Blessed Sacrament."[11]

The more we turn our attention Godward, the more our eyes grow accustomed to recognizing the risen Lord in our ordinary walks of life. We develop "ears of the heart" by listening for the Lord's voice in the midst of all the other voices clamoring for our attention. Some days, we are given the grace to see Christ in the visage of our child or spouse; other days, God's presence seems obscure. But we cannot simply "will" such perception; it comes as a gift and evolves gradually as the Spirit trains us in receptivity to God's mysterious ways. The practice of simple but specific disciplines of prayer prepares us for a more general and encompassing practice of God's presence in life.

Most parents can recall times when God's presence became suddenly apparent through some family incident, unexpected question, or surprising pronouncement from a child. One of our godchildren was only three when a recording by Mozart caught her full attention. Her parents asked if she knew who had written the music; in a hushed and solemn tone, the child responded, "God." Her theologically literate parents were duly edified!

Children often say more than they know. One of my favorite stories of child wisdom comes from a Methodist pastor whose son had excitedly recounted to his father what he learned in Sunday school that morning. The boy took his father to their scenic window overlooking an extended yard and said, "God is bigger than our whole house and bigger than our whole yard!" The father, who couldn't resist a little theological correction, said, "Yes, Matthew, that's true; but you know, God also lives in our hearts." Matthew was silent at this baffling new information. A few days later, as his father tucked him into bed, he protested, "But, Daddy, if God lives inside our hearts, why aren't our hearts bursting?" *Why, indeed!* his father wondered.[12]

The young child's evident delight in simple pleasures we have long since taken for granted can reawaken us to the wonder of life itself. A friend wrote this to me when her first child was almost two: "Having a child is an experience of *savoring* life— the small things and the things we have come to know so well that we have forgotten about them—the fun of splashing water, the way little green peas roll around the dinner plate!" Not only can our children lead us to what Lawrence Ferlinghetti calls "a rebirth of wonder," but their focused attention on the moment can renew our capacity for contemplative presence. Contemplation has much to do with sinking into the present moment with our full attention and enjoyment. Moments of contemplation seem timeless, and children seem to live naturally in such moments.

I believe there is a valid distinction to be made between natural contemplation and the contemplation of God, however. In the latter, our attention is focused consciously on God's presence and is, in some sense, genuinely an experience of the eternal. Yet even if the subject of contemplation differs, the basic capacity is the same, and we can move gradually toward the contemplation of God through awareness of the divine presence in our natural contemplation. A colleague of my husband once mused that he found it impossible to understand how a monk could spend hours in silent contemplation before the Reserved Sacrament. His son, whose wife had just given birth to their first child, responded immediately that he could understand it quite well. He found that he could spend hours just looking at their newborn infant, completely entranced by the tiny form and face. The child did not need to be awake or make any movement at all to absorb his new father's rapt attention. The very moment this young father sees the wonder of God present *through* the wonder of his child, the contemplation of God has sprung forth from natural contemplation.

## Supporting One Another's Solitude

There are ways to support and encourage the innate human capacity for contemplation. One of the simplest and most central of these is to protect quiet time and space within family life. Every person, even the most extroverted, needs some time alone. Family life, with its intimate proximities, can make both time and space difficult to find. It is ideal if children have their own rooms to retreat to and if spouses have an extra room such as a study for personal space. But in many households such space is a luxury. Some families have found a creative solution by setting up one corner of a common room with a comfortable chair where members may go if they want to be quiet. When a person occupies that chair, the desire to be left alone is understood and respected.

Some families have quiet times during which children are expected to play quietly by themselves while adults rest, read, or relax. It is best if such a tradition is established early on, so that even young children accept a limited time period in which they do not interrupt their parents or siblings except in real need. Perhaps the easiest way to establish such time is to connect it with naps at the beginning of a child's life. Once children are in school, quiet time can still be valuable to the family on weekends. In this way, children learn to attach a positive value to silence and solitude within the home. If time alone in one's room is used solely as a threat or punishment, the result can be a negative experience of solitude that undermines the capacity for prayer.[13]

Family support for individual solitude need not be restricted to the home environment. There are times when each member will need to get away. Family interactions can be intense, conflictual, and sometimes suffocating; but even when they are not, times of absence from one another can renew the deeper bonds of relationship. Even the best marriage needs a component of solitude for each partner, which can be met both within and beyond the home. Children need opportunities for solitude beyond the home as well, especially as they grow older, perhaps through nature camps or church retreats. Not only absence itself, but the maturation that occurs through such experiences can help to revitalize family relationships.

Honoring the need for solitude creates sufficient space in a family for healthy, nonpossessive relationships to develop. It also creates adequate space for the comfort of friends and visitors, and so supports the family practice of hospitality.

Indeed, the discipline of prayer with its ability to release us from illusions, to foster a contemplative awareness of God's presence, and to help us honor one another's solitude undergirds every other form of family ministry.

## *For Reflection*

⁓Do you experience prayer as central to family life? If so, how?

⁓What are some of the barriers you encounter to praying at home, both as an individual and as a family?

⁓Which forms of prayer suggested in this chapter particularly appeal to you? Which seem well suited to overcoming the barriers you have identified?

⁓When have you become aware of God's presence in the midst of ordinary activities or situations in your family life?

⁓How do you, or how might you, support the need for silence or solitude at home?

# 6

# Celebrating God's Presence

_The core of a celebration speaks to the hearts of all humankind—in all times and in all places. It speaks the symbolic language of the soul and is hardly ever practical, but more poetic, playful, prayerful. . . . Ceremony makes the ordinary extraordinary._

—Gertrud Mueller Nelson[1]

THE MORE ATTUNED WE BECOME to the divine presence through prayer, the more every detail of our life together can be lived as a celebration of that presence. Becoming conscious of God's spirit in the ordinary routines of our day and learning to respond take time and practice. That is the significance of particular disciplines like family worship, seasonal rituals, and special celebrations. The practice of Sabbath-keeping and genuine recreation also is given us as a means of becoming attuned to the divine presence in life and learning to respond with reverence and joy.

Children need to see that the spiritual life is significant to their parents at home as well as at church. Otherwise the artificial dichotomy between faith and life that marks the modern church is reinforced and perpetuated. Children need to see their parents setting time aside for prayer, worship, reflection, and open discussion about issues of faith. "Without modeling, children may not be inspired to give expression to their own spiritual lives."[2]

## Family Worship

Families may celebrate the presence of God in the midst of everyday life in innumerable ways. The previous discussion of the importance of concrete images, signs, and symbols in a child's spiritual development may lead us to ask what kind of tangible symbols or visual images we have in our homes that speak of faith. Have we any religious art? I have in mind profound and powerful art, not the sentimental images common to religious culture. Is there a "sacred space" set aside for worship with a few simple symbols of our faith in it?

Some families have a little table set like an altar with a Bible, a candle, and perhaps a beautiful icon or homemade cross. It can be a place for spontaneous offerings: wildflowers, autumn leaves, a speckled egg, a bright feather, or other treasures collected while exploring. Parents might encourage children to collect symbols from some parables: a mustard seed from the spice rack (Matt. 13:31-32), an interesting coin (Luke 15:8-10), an artificial pearl or a white marble for the "pearl of great price" (Matt. 13:45-46). These would have their special place on or near the altar and could be used in family worship and scriptural reflection. Families might cut out figures or create clay figurines to depict shepherd and sheep or a Christmas crèche. Cavalletti reports that children love to play with such figures and can spend remarkable periods of time contemplating biblical stories with the aid of concrete objects. Over time, and through play, they will gradually assimilate biblical meanings.

The child's need for concrete objects and physical activity in learning is part of why ritual in family worship is so essential. Rituals are embodied ways of celebrating God's presence in the midst of ordinary life. They take the common stuff of life and reveal its sacramental capacity. Always include some ritual expression in family worship rather than remain in the realm of abstract words. Adults, like children, respond inwardly to the power of symbols and actions in worship.

A family ritual can be as simple as the ancient Jewish meal blessing in which a glass of wine (or juice) is blessed and passed from one family member to another, followed by bread blessed and shared in like manner. The simple act of lighting a candle can turn prayer or scripture reading into a ritual. Children respond favorably to the Advent wreath ritual, especially if practiced faithfully through the season. The making of special foods and colorful decorations for particular seasons of the church year can be ritualized with a few simple songs or prayers. Singing hymns and songs of faith together, gathered around one or two musical instruments, can itself become a joyous family ritual.

Family worship is an important expression of celebrating God's presence in the midst of home life. It need not be long or formal, only regular. Although some people may be more comfortable with special periodic family worship, a daily practice simple enough to be feasible has much to recommend it. Morning and evening prayer in the home have a long and venerable history.

All great religious traditions have practiced the observance of prayer at specific hours of the day to keep people mindful of God's presence in ordinary time. It was common Jewish practice to offer morning and evening sacrifice at the Temple and to pray at midmorning and midafternoon. Dividing the day into hours and establishing a natural rhythm of prayer have been carried on by Christians through many centuries, particularly in monastic communities. The Reformers encouraged congregations to practice morning and evening prayer as a daily corporate discipline. But in Protestantism the family became the focal point for the practice of morning and evening prayer: "By the end of the sixteenth century, it was common for families to gather each morning to begin the day with prayer. At the evening dinner table, following the meal, the family would sing a psalm, listen to scripture, and join in prayer, the essential ingredients in any service of daily prayer."[3] Other times for personal prayer were specified as well. Calvin recommended prayer on arising, before work, at meals, and on retiring at night.

The idea of incorporating morning and evening prayer into our busy family lives may seem somewhat daunting. But there are simple and natural ways to establish such a practice, especially when children are young. It is ideal if parents already have some kind of regular daily worship together in which young children can be included as a matter of course. Naturally as children grow, the level of their participation and perhaps the structure of family worship itself will change.

One family I know has enjoyed a simple process for morning prayer that has held its appeal for many years. When gathered for breakfast, members share what the coming day holds for them—both what they look forward to and what they are anxious about. Then each family member prays briefly for the others. Not only do family members feel heard, supported, and cared for before leaving home each morning, but they remember one another at critical hours of the day and are eager to find out how things have gone when they gather again for supper.

For a more structured and scripturally based approach to family worship, a variety of good resources are available. One of my favorites is the *Book of Common Worship: Daily Prayer.*[4] It offers simple morning and evening prayer services for every season of the church year and can be adapted easily for the family setting. Evening prayer is especially good because it incorporates the ancient service of light with a hymn of light and the lighting of a candle. The resource includes a daily lectionary, the entire psalter with psalm tones and refrains, mealtime graces, a fine selection of litanies and prayers—including prayers for the family and personal life—along with helpful introductions and instructions. One of the beauties of this resource is that it is also intended for corporate use within the larger church and its various fellowship groupings. When the same form of prayer is used in settings such as church meetings or retreats *and* at home, family members are more likely to experience their home prayer as integrally connected to the prayer of the whole faith community.

It seems fitting to mention here that family recreation in the natural world is a special way of celebrating God's presence with us, and can be experienced as a rich expression of worship. The need for natural recreation in our time is underscored by the speed with which the human race is depleting and degrading the earth's finite resources. Children who are allowed plenty of play in natural settings are more likely to develop a deep respect for the earth and its creatures than those who are deprived of such recreation. Family camping or holidays spent visiting scenic national preserves can reinforce a sense of responsible stewardship for the increasingly fragile, unified ecosystem we call earth. Time spent in nature seems almost universally to elicit a sense of the holiness and awesomeness of life. It is a gift that draws from us natural reverence and worship. Many people, adults and children alike, feel God's presence more fully in the beauty and grandeur of the natural creation than in any other setting. It is a gift worth celebrating and preserving!

## Seasonal Rituals

Some of the most effective practices for nurturing family spirituality are ritual celebrations. We have noted the importance of ritual expression in family worship and how it can help reveal the sacramental dimension of ordinary life. A ritual is an intentional ceremony, a repeatable rite that uses symbolic acts with or without words to express and carry the meaning of our faith.

Author Gertrud Mueller Nelson speaks of watching small children at the sea, enacting an age-old ritual. Faced with something as overwhelming as the ocean, they turn their backs and dig a hole in the sand that allows a small part of the sea to enter. This mini-sea is comprehensible and can be played with, even while the unpredictable ocean waves swamp it and require more digging. Like children faced with the imponderables of the mighty ocean, we humans create rituals that enable us to live with the overwhelming reality of God. Ritual gives form to the formless Spirit; gives intelligible names, patterns, and rhythms to the infinite mystery of the divine presence.[5]

In family life we may have *daily* rituals, such as mealtime graces, bedtime stories, morning and evening prayer, or some of the forms of prayer we described in chapter 5. The primary *weekly* ritual of faith for most families is Sunday worship. But I would like to focus here on *seasonal* rituals in the home. Families of faith can reclaim holidays for the Holy Days they were intended to be. Let's look briefly at each of the following celebrations: Advent-Christmas, Lent-Easter, Halloween-All Saints Day, and Valentine's Day.

## *Advent-Christmas*

Advent has tremendous significance for Christians. It is the *beginning* of the church year, characterized by expectation and longing for the coming of God's promised Messiah. Advent is a season of preparation for the joy of the Incarnation. But many people, including good church folk, experience little joy in Christmas these days. We should not be surprised if we don't experience real joy in Christmas when we do not engage in the serious and intentional preparation of Advent.

The problem is that Advent does not exist in our culture. Thanks to the juggernaut of commercial profit, the season of Advent has been replaced by a Christmas season now imposed upon us well before Thanksgiving. The choice to let Advent be Advent can only be made and held to in our churches and homes because public space is thoroughly co-opted by consumer mentality and commercial interests.

I believe that even in our churches and homes, it is only possible to reclaim Advent to the extent that we change our way of perceiving and celebrating Christmas. If Christmas is understood *primarily* as a time for gift-giving, elaborate parties, and meeting our children's expectations of goods and goodies, Advent has little chance of reemerging. It will remain, of necessity, the great party and purchase frenzy of the year.

The question our faith asks of us during Advent is, "How do we prepare ourselves spiritually for God's self-gift to us in Christ?" As we consider how we might best honor the Word made flesh for us, some fitting responses might be worship and adoration, repentance and amendment of life, or expressions of love for the least and the lost. How might we start focusing on these aspects of Advent in the home? Here are a few practical suggestions:

~ Spend the day after Thanksgiving making your own family Advent calendar instead of buying into the biggest sales day of the year at your local mall. Get the whole family involved. Write into the space behind each daily window: a scripture passage to read and reflect on as a family; or a suggestion of some person / group to pray for; or an act of kindness for the day (write a letter to someone who lives alone; take canned goods to the local food pantry; do something nice for your sister, brother, spouse, parent, or grandparent). Such a calendar gives a special family activity for each day of Advent, encouraging communication, prayer, and generosity.

~ Decide as a family that you will simplify your giving for Christmas. Write a letter to your extended family to explain your choice and invite them to join you. Consider alternate ways of giving that relate to your time or talent: the promise of a day at the park together or a special Saturday with each of your children as they would most enjoy it (perhaps a museum or zoo trip or a day spent fishing) A few years ago when my brother was without a job for a stretch, he gave his wife the gift of a repainted kitchen—a Christmas present accomplished in the spring. A handmade gift or a personal poem might be the most meaningful thing we could give someone. Encourage children to use their creative talents to make gifts for their parents or siblings. If parents can set aside a few special evenings to help their children with gift-making, it becomes an opportunity for special bonding during Advent.

~ Help children recover the "saint" in Santa Claus. Our churches could teach us the story of Saint Nicholas, whose anonymous generosity was the original model for our version of the jolly old elf himself. Some families teach that Saint Nicholas still lives in the hearts of mothers and fathers and children who catch onto his message and participate in his secret giving. The spirit of Nicholas inspires how we prepare our gifts and the spirit in which we give and receive. It fills the house with mysterious and unseen secrets, so that each of us becomes "a little Nicholas," sneaking around and doing good turns for one another without ever letting on "whodunit."[6]

## *Lent-Easter*

Like Advent, Lent is a season of spiritual preparation for the consummate joy of the Christian year, Easter. Again the true joy of Easter will be lost on us if we do not seriously engage the opportunity Lent presents us with. Thankfully, Easter is far less commercialized than Christmas, which gives Lent a fighting chance. Gertrud Mueller Nelson points out that the traditional disciplines of Lent offer us a holistic experience of the spiritual life. There is prayer for the soul, fasting for the body, and almsgiving for the neighbor.[7] Let's look briefly at each in turn.

Lent is an excellent time to introduce family members to the practice of self-examination in private and family prayer. Churches might offer a pre-Lenten workshop on the classic practice of "examen of conscience" and the more modern "examination of consciousness."[8] The former has a more distinctly confessional cast, and the latter is similar to the "glad, sad, sorry prayer times." Families can adapt this prayer form to their own situation, encouraging self-examination at the end of each day, whether individually or together.

Fasting is a discipline we desperately need to recover in a culture where food is so plentiful and cheap that we can both glorify and trivialize it. Families can decide together on ways to simplify their food intake during Lent, learning to experience the spiritual dimension of the season in their bodies as well as their minds and hearts. Cutting out rich and unnecessary foods is the basic intent of Lenten fasting. But other forms of abstinence might be appropriate to consider also. What would it mean, for example, to fast from overconsumption of clothes, videos, or gadgets? What would it be like to fast from recognition (practicing anonymity)? What about abstaining from gossip, from judging others, or from overcommitting our schedules? If you want to know the most appropriate forms of fasting for you, ask yourself the question "What do I do to excess?"[9]

Mueller Nelson has a lovely suggestion for almsgiving during Lent. Her family keeps a box on the dining table, inscribed around by the words, *The Fasts of the Rich Are the Feasts of the Poor*.[10] Into the box goes whatever money family members save during Lent by foregoing desserts or better cuts of meat or movies or by making lunches instead of eating out. The family decides each year which charity or humane cause the alms box collection will support.

After the cleansing astringency of Lent, our bodies can participate in Easter joy by feasting on some of the rich foods that we have abstained from for six weeks. It is a wonderful tradition to have special foods that are only eaten Easter day, just as we have many special foods that are specific to Christmas. Children can be taught that Easter eggs, chicks, and bunnies all symbolize the new life that is made possible for us through Jesus' resurrection. Even new clothes are meant to symbolize new life in Christ, a reminder of our baptism in which we take off the garment of our "old life" and become "clothed in Christ" (Eph. 4:22-24). Of course adults and older children don't need whole new outfits every year. A new item of clothing is symbolic. Catholic social activist Dorothy Day once got a new pair of shoelaces for Easter, and that sufficiently delighted her!

Easter also can be recovered as a *season* that begins with the day of Resurrection. Family prayer and worship can reflect this. A special Easter candle, symbolizing the light of our risen Lord, can be used in family worship throughout the season. Because it corresponds with spring, the Easter season is an especially good time for the family to get out into the beauties of the natural world to enjoy the newness of creation.

### Halloween-All Saints' Day

Halloween is All Hallows' Eve, the night before All Saints' Day. Some churches still celebrate All Saints' Day, but few help us make the connection with All Hallows' Eve. It is traditionally the night in which the minions of death and the devil come out in force to wreak whatever havoc they may before their powers are eclipsed by the mighty force of all God's saints. Behind this old tradition lies a mixture of the fear of evil and a fear of the mystery of death (legends of souls hovering about the earth in the form of ghosts). Yet All Saints' Day expresses faith in the greater power of God's goodness that overcomes evil and God's life that transcends death.

Might this not suggest that Halloween and All Saints' Day would be good times to talk with our children about death in relation to our faith? This holiday presents an opportunity to express our natural fears and feelings of loss concerning death but also our hope and faith in entrusting ourselves to Christ in death. All Saints' Day is an excellent time to pull out the old family picture albums and talk about our ancestors.

It would be a good time to tend family graves, to recall family and friends who have died, remembering their contributions to life. It is a good time to talk about how we would like to be remembered or to tell stories about the lives of the saints we most admire.[11] How many parents these days would think to read the story of a great saint to their children on All Saints' Day? How many of us would engage in a conversation about modern or even living saints? Who would we identify as a saint, and why?

## *Valentine's Day*

There are many saints we would do well to remember with celebration. Why, then, don't we teach the legend of Saint Valentine? He was a third-century Christian, imprisoned for defending his beliefs. The jailer's daughter visited him faithfully every day until his execution. In his parting note to her, Valentine thanked her for her friendship and kindness, signing simply, "Your Valentine." It was an expression of *agape* love and friendship, a far cry from the winged cupids of Eros that decorate our greeting cards today. Might it not be appropriate to honor the spirit of Christ in this saint by visiting someone in prison? by writing a letter to encourage a prisoner of conscience through Amnesty International? by working toward forgiveness or reconciliation with someone to whom you need to be reconciled? by talking with a person of another faith in order to gain understanding of their beliefs and traditions? Any one of these may be encouraged within the home setting.

These holidays are only a few that we may reclaim as holy days. Let me urge you to put on your collective family "thinking hats" about ways to celebrate Thanksgiving or Saint Patrick's Day, for example, in a manner that lifts up the spiritual import of

the festivities. You might surprise yourselves with the fresh
ideas that get generated!

# Unique Rites of Life Passage

Families also can be encouraged to create home celebrations for
some of the more unique rituals that belong to our faith tradition.
The church celebrates several life-passage points that are closely
related to family growth and therefore lend themselves to home
celebration—unique, once-in-a-lifetime events like baptism, confirmation, marriage, and death.

## *Baptism*

Eastern Orthodox Christians traditionally wait until baptism to
name their children, and rather than celebrating natural birthdays
they celebrate baptismal anniversaries. One of my seminary pro-
fessors was fond of pointing out that children know what is important to us by what we regularly celebrate.

If we believe that baptism marks the promise of our new
identity in Christ, why do we not celebrate our baptismal anniversaries with as much joy and festivity as we do natural birthdays? It would certainly be appropriate for churches to remember the anniversaries of their members' spiritual birth. But what
of the domestic church? Might we consider celebrating our children's baptismal anniversaries at home, perhaps sharing the occasion with church friends or the child's godparents? We might
tell children the story of their baptism with accompanying
pictures, just as we recite the story of their birth. Make a tape of
the baptismal service and play it on each anniversary. Some
churches give a large candle to the parents at their child's
baptism to be taken home and lit each year, commemorating the
child's welcome into the Body of Christ.

I was once told of parents who asked their children before
each baptismal anniversary, "Who has been most important in
your faith life this year?" Sometimes the child would identify
someone who lived far away but who had visited or written. On
one occasion, the person named was not a member of any
church. The parents invited this special mentor to share a

baptismal celebration in their home. Often this shared experience was as meaningful to the person invited as to the child.

For those of you who have been baptized as adults or who can consciously recall the event as a young person, remembering your baptism will already have special personal meaning. Yet those in the "believer's baptism" tradition still need to celebrate this significant decision for faith annually. Gather a community of believers around you, tell the story of how you came to be a Christian, and celebrate your baptismal anniversary in the most appropriate and meaningful way you can imagine.

## *Confirmation*

For those who were baptized as infants, confirmation is meant to be the moment of believing affirmation that would parallel believer's baptism. Yet when I was growing up, many of my peers experienced confirmation as a rather dull exercise. What could have been a major initiation into the adult life and membership responsibilities of the church had been diluted into a few anemic classes. The solemn, brief ceremony in church made no symbolic connection to baptism and ended up marking little more, for many youngsters, than the eagerly awaited end of church attendance in deference to parental pressure.

Thankfully more churches are now helping young people make the connection between their baptism and confirmation. Many confirmation classes require serious learning and evidence of personal assimilation of the faith. Yet a generation after my own experience, I found a colleague telling me how disappointed her twelve-year-old son had been with his confirmation process. The boy lamented that their church had nothing comparable to the bar mitzvahs he was experiencing with his Jewish friends. A bar mitzvah or bas mitzvah require the recital of lengthy memorized portions of the Hebrew Scriptures and a substantial statement of the meaning of faith in one's own words.

Perhaps the greater difference lies in the family dimension of a bar mitzvah or bas mitzvah. In the Jewish community, this rite of passage into adulthood is marked not only by the temple or synagogue service but by a great celebrative party, where parents, siblings, and close friends may speak honest and often humorous words about the maturation they have witnessed in this child-becoming-adult. By contrast, confirmation often represents a church ritual with little corresponding support from home or family.

How might Christian families celebrate the confirmation of their children as a true rite of passage into the early adulthood of their faith? Perhaps a family-and-friends party could be part of such a celebration. It would not need to be elaborate or expensive in order to communicate real meaning and joy. The faith of the young person would need to be lifted up in some central way, perhaps through the recitation of memorized psalms or other portions of scripture or by having the confirmand offer the meal blessing. Some simple family prayers and rituals especially for this occasion would be important.

As the church welcomes young people into the adult responsibilities of the church, parents can reinforce that passage into adulthood by adding certain privileges and responsibilities within the home. One family took their daughters to a special restaurant after the confirmation service and initiated them into greater fiscal responsibility at home. Henceforth the daughters would receive a lump sum each month rather than a weekly allowance. They were then responsible for buying their own clothes and taking care of incidental personal expenses. If they ran out of money before the end of the month, they would receive no handouts. Before those girls graduated from high school, they were able to travel abroad and handle their finances with complete confidence and competence. They had learned fiscal responsibility. It was an exercise in good stewardship that their parents had connected to the rite of confirmation.

## *Marriage*

The church has something substantial to offer family health in the arena of marriage. Here we move toward what the church needs to do to prepare and support family spirituality, a topic that will be addressed more directly in the final chapter. A solid marriage remains the preferred foundation and backbone of healthy family life.

What theology of marriage does the church teach? The church needs to lift up the uniqueness of its view of marriage in a culture drowning in secular understandings of marriage. Romantic love—the love our cultural myths proclaim as absolutely indispensable to marriage—is based on the illusion that one other person can meet all my personal and emotional needs. Christian love is based on something more substantial: loyalty, fidelity of relationship, a love that seeks to serve the other and is ready to relinquish personal desires for the sake of the other's good. Christian love is grounded in God's sacrificial love for us. While more demanding than romantic love, it is infinitely more real and fulfilling!

Beyond this dimension of commitment, perhaps the great uniqueness of Christian marriage lies in its vision of marriage as a *vocation*, a calling. A Christian marriage occurs when two persons are called together by God to be a witness to and a reflection of God's faithful, forgiving, and fruitful love. Christian marriage is not merely a matter of mutual attraction, common interest, or compatibility—much less simple romantic love—though all of these may be important elements in the vitality of married life.

God calls two people together to learn how to love with God's love in the midst of the inevitable pressures and projections of an intimate relationship. Christian marriage is a way of knowing God more fully through one particular, committed relationship of love. It expresses the mystery of learning universal love through practicing with one. Therefore such intimacy does not exist merely for its own sake, but for the sake of witness to a world God loves. I recall Henri Nouwen once saying, "Intimacy does not consist of gazing infinitely into each others' eyes, but of looking outward together in the same direction."

How might families help honor and celebrate the central place of marriage in their life together? Wedding anniversaries are commonly celebrated by couples and their families already, yet few celebrations lift up the sacred dimension of marriage in our culture.

For many years, my husband and I played a tape of our wedding service on each anniversary and made a practice of renewing our vows to each other. We continue to enjoy remembering stories of people and events surrounding our marriage each year. An anniversary is a good time for a couple to spend some time discerning what God is calling them to grow toward and witness to. For major markers such as a twenty-fifth or fiftieth anniversary, some couples ask their pastor to help them with a renewal of wedding vows service. Every such service I have participated in has been deeply meaningful to all involved.

## *Death*

What does the church teach its children about death? We have touched on this subject in our consideration of All Hallows' Eve and All Saints' Day, but I would like to carry our thoughts further. We live in a culture that assiduously avoids and denies death. The subject is, in many cases, deemed altogether inappropriate for children. Yet at the same time, our culture is full of death and violence—from television, movies, heavy metal and rap music to the realities of the drug culture and teen suicide. In terms of faith, children are often left to pick up what they can from scripture or sermons, while few adults will talk with them directly about death.

Death is a great mystery to all of us, not just to children. They know quite well how we feel about dying; what they want and deserve to know from us is what we believe about it. If as Christians we have nothing significant and hopeful to offer our children on the subject of death, we are cheating them of the birthright of their faith and ourselves as well.

Families are natural settings to teach children a faith perspective on death and life. The death of a family pet often elicits the child's natural desire for a ritual that serves to express feelings, to capture the meaning of the pet in the family's life, and to mark a final good-bye. Encourage (but do not force) children to attend memorial services if a person dies with whom they have had a special relationship—especially a grandparent, close relative, or family friend. Feelings of sadness and grief need acknowledgment and sharing. It is damaging, both emotionally and physically, to hold feelings of grief inside without expressing them. Celebrate the deceased person's life and gifts; be honest about his or her weaknesses as well. Faith in God's power to forgive and to resurrect should be central and visible!

I hope you will find here enough suggestions to spark your own creative impulse for ritual-making, whether it be connected to family worship, holidays, or life-passage points. Human beings are born to worship God. Seasons of the human life cycle, seasons of the church calendar, and seasons of the natural world that shape our daily life all claim legitimate rights to family celebration. Explore and enjoy your creative capacities!

## *For Reflection*

～ How does your family celebrate God's presence in daily life?

～ What forms of family worship seem practical to you?

～ Do you practice making holidays into Holy Days? Which ideas described in this chapter appeal to you?

～ How would you like to celebrate unique rites of passage in your home setting?

# 7

# The Family as Storyteller and Guide

~

*And these words which I command you this day shall be
upon your heart; and you shall teach them diligently to
your children, and shall talk of them when you sit in your
house, and when you walk by the way, and when you lie
down, and when you rise.*

—Deuteronomy 6:6-7, RSV

*Do not forget the things your eyes have seen, nor let them
slip from your heart all the days of your life; rather, tell
them to your children and to your children's children.*

—Deuteronomy 4:9, JB

FAMILIES ARE NATURAL PURVEYORS of stories.
Children love nothing more than to climb into the lap
of a parent who is ready to tell them a story. For
Christians, one great story encompasses all other
stories—the good news. Scripture tells the great story from
beginning to end: from the creation of all that is, through the
covenant promises made to Israel, to the fulfillment of those
promises in Jesus, and on to the promised culmination of Jesus'
risen life in the kingdom of God. It is a story full of drama,
realism, mystery, and power—a story that engages us to the core

103

because the dynamics of human sin and divine faithfulness speak to our condition as truly now as they did when the stories of the Bible were first told.

Knowledge of scripture is as indispensable a foundation for the Christian life as prayer. Indeed, the study of scripture and the practice of prayer are inseparable. It is through scripture that we know our identity as people of faith, and through the Gospels in particular that we know our Christian identity. Since Christian theology and practice have their roots in the life story of Jesus Christ, the Gospels are the center from which Christians read both Old and New Testaments. Here alone we find a record of the life and teachings of the One whose name we bear.

Scripture itself is a record of corporate memory and practice known as tradition. The Hebrew Scriptures reveal how Israel, through many centuries and many representative voices, understood herself in relation to the one true God. The identity of Israel was intrinsically bound to her history with this God, a history passed down orally through generations and remembered in cyclical community celebrations and family rituals long before it was recorded on parchment. The scrolls merely preserved Israel's experience of divine revelation and her corporate memory in written form. New Testament stories, interpretations, and traditions were also preserved in memory and community practices before being committed to writing.

The church is the prime bearer of this corporate memory, drawing on the ancient traditions and practices that helped to shape the canon of scripture itself and returning to scripture over the course of centuries to correct and reshape its tradition and practice.

Church families, as domestic expressions of the greater whole, are also called to be carriers of corporate memory. There are three levels of story relevant to our faith that the family can tell: personal stories, family-ancestral stories, and biblical stories. The family is in a unique position to integrate these three levels. One of the most critical functions of family storytelling is to help its members make connections between their personal stories and God's great story.

Communities of people have engaged in this kind of biblical identification for centuries. The black church in America has seen in the story of the Exodus a central metaphor for its own pilgrimage from slavery to freedom. Black Christians have found their life experience reflected in the oppression of the Israelites in Egypt, and the Promised Land remains an image of hope for complete liberation from continued forms of economic and social bondage. Thus, the history and experience of the black church are interpreted and wonderfully encompassed (though not exhausted) by the story of the Exodus.

In Latin America, marginalized Christians have found a central metaphor in the crucified Christ. Jesus is a man of sorrows and affliction like their own. God is preeminently the One who suffers out of love and whose suffering gathers up the sufferings of all who hunger and thirst for righteousness. The Resurrection signifies the long-awaited reversal of human values and order, the exoneration of the last who shall be first and the least who shall be greatest in the kingdom of heaven. Thus, the historical experience of oppressed Christians in Latin America receives meaning through the story of Jesus' crucifixion and resurrection.

Like larger communities with particular histories, families may also discover certain stories of scripture that seem to speak vividly to their condition, reflecting their struggles and offering hope. Yet in a fundamental sense, for Christians the norm will always be the cross and the empty tomb. Indeed the story of the Exodus, with its movement from bondage to freedom, prefigures what lies at the heart of the passion and resurrection of Jesus. The shape of the Christian life, as noted in the first chapter, is cruciform. Death to the old life of bondage to sin and rebirth to the new life of freedom in Christ is the central dynamic of any life incorporated into Christ.

Since these dynamics are at the core of individual Christian experience, we can expect them to occur in families of faith, as in any relationships among church members. A family that is really growing experiences a constant ebb and flow of loss and new hope. Age, self-image, feelings, the nature of relationships, efforts to control or let go—these factors are shifting continually within family life. In homes of faith where conscious spiritual growth is valued, these changing dynamics need to be named and understood within the framework of death and new life in Christ.

One of the beauties of scripture is that we can find ourselves in its stories in fresh ways throughout a lifetime. We may identify with different characters at various stages of life. We may also identify with the same character in different ways over time, discovering a new depth or unexpected trait in the biblical figure because of changed self-perception or life circumstance. If we approach scripture as a living word, we will find that it both embraces and expands our own experience.

## The Great Story: God's Word

We find our lives taken into and transformed by the Word for good reason. Two meanings of God's Word are familiar to us. The first is *scripture* as a unique witness to the creating and re-creating Word of God among God's covenant people; the second is the culmination and fulfillment of scripture in the Word incarnate, *Jesus Christ*. Robert Mulholland suggests yet a third meaning. Each of us is also a word of God, "spoken forth" into being with a glorious purpose in Christ "before the foundation of the world" (Eph. 1:4).[1] Even though we now are "garbled, distorted and debased" words, our destiny in Christ is to be redeemed and conformed to the image in which we were made.

Mulholland's interpretation suggests that there are innate connections between God's Word in scripture, the incarnate Word, and the word God speaks us forth to be. It has been said that God has promised to encounter us in two settings: scripture and our own life stories. If this is so, Jesus' life represents the fulfillment of each and the perfect expression of how they are joined. We are transformed in and by the incarnate Word, present to us in the sacraments and in the written word through the working of the Holy Spirit.

The mystery in the written word goes beyond the mere recording of a people's historical self-understanding. Just as God's spirit brooded over a nascent creation, God brooded over tiny Israel, shaping experience, memory, and hope into an oral and written record that could well be termed a "verbal icon" of God's kingdom.[2] An icon is a window between two realities; it participates in and mediates between two worlds, interpreting the human condition to God and interpreting God's vision to humankind. What this means is that the words of scripture "read us" as much as we read them. A reality behind the words encounters and addresses us.

When the Book of Hebrews declares, "The Word of God is living and active . . . able to judge the thoughts and intentions of the heart" (4:12, NASB), it indicates that God's Word penetrates and discerns us, even while we imagine ourselves penetrating the meaning of the text! God's Word reveals us to ourselves as we really are, uncovering our mixed motives and our astonishing array of rationalizations. This quality of scripture allows it to transform us inwardly. That is why attentive listening to God's Word in scripture is one of the primary disciplines of the spiritual life. If we would be conformed to the image of Christ, the living Word, we need time to allow God's Word to transform us.

## Making the Word Our Home

The Gospel of John offers a scriptural image for this process of transformation. Jesus says, "If you make my word your home you will indeed be my disciples, you will learn the truth and the truth will make you free" (8:31-32, JB). Chapter 15 picks up the metaphor of God's Word as "home": "Make your home in me, as I make mine in you. . . . If you remain in me and my words remain in you, you may ask what you will and you shall get it" (vv. 4, 7, JB).

What does it mean to make God's Word our home or dwelling place? To begin with, at home we are familiar with all the rooms, furnishings, pictures, and other appointments. In order to be at home in the Word, we need to be familiar with the content of scripture in all its diversity and cohesion. At home we also are accustomed to the peculiar rhythms, patterns, and rituals of family life within it. To be at home with God's Word involves familiarity with the patterns of life and worship of the community that lives within the framework of its content—the church. Part of being at home in a place is knowing the views from all the windows and knowing how doors connect one room to another. Part of being at home in God's Word is knowing how we view the world from within its faith perspective—the angle of vision God's love gives us on life—as well as understanding how its theological views are connected internally.

How, within the home, do we make the Word our "home"? The stories, parables, prophecies, and psalms of scripture need to be read, reflected on, and discussed within the family. Families can structure the reading and hearing of scripture into family life in many ways. If morning and evening prayers are made as much a part of family time as meals and recreation, daily lections can help readily build the walls of our dwelling place with God.

One family I know practices a simple evening discipline around God's Word. The children in this family were very young when my husband and I first joined them for an evening meal. After supper, the father read a portion of scripture while the mother attended their infant daughter and a two-year-old son moved quietly around the table. Following the reading, a brief prayer was offered. The whole thing took less than five minutes. No great effort was made to keep the baby completely quiet or to stifle the natural movement of the little boy.

About three years later we had occasion to share supper in the home of this family again. This time, as his father began reading the scripture passage, the now five-year-old boy piped up, "Daddy, let me tell it!" He proceeded to render a very accurate paraphrase of the story in his own simple vocabulary. What impressed us most was that simply hearing the stories of scripture, day after day over time, had brought this child to a state of biblical literacy in a natural way. Of course he received reinforcement from worship and schooling at church, and no doubt there had been conversations at home about some of the stories and passages read. However, without the daily discipline of home worship, this child probably would not have known or cared to tell the story as he did.

Another way to incorporate learning the Bible at home is to read from a good paraphrase of scripture for bedtime stories. One of the best I know is called *The Children's Bible*, which puts the great biblical stories into easily understood language, yet remains faithful to the movement and details of scripture.[3]

## The Preeminent Place of the Psalms

The psalms hold a special place in the worship life of the church. Psalms has aptly been called "the prayer book of the Bible," having formed the center of liturgical and personal prayer for both Jews and Christians over the course of centuries. No book of the Bible expresses such a wide range of human emotion. These hymns and poems give voice to praise, wonder, thanksgiving, anguish, doubt, fear, fury, contrition, trust, and hope — sometimes moving through several feelings in one psalm. Because they "commerce in raw emotion,"[4] the psalms can be troubling or problematic to many people of faith. Yet the more willing we are to acknowledge honestly the feelings that emerge so forcefully from within us and to express them to God, the more meaningful the psalms become. They give us not only permission but words to voice the most sublime and tumultuous depths of the heart in prayer.

In periods of stress and turmoil, these ancient prayers may strike deep chords of recognition for family members. Dolores Leckey writes of how valuable the psalms proved to be at a particular stage in her family's life: "During the children's adolescence we relied on the Psalms for our evening prayer: one Psalm and a ritual grace. I think the young men and women around our dinner table appreciated being carried along by something older, wiser, and stronger than themselves."[5] Psalms of praise and thanksgiving may be especially helpful for younger children, since thanks and adoration seem to be the native form of prayer for children under six years of age.

Churches rarely teach youngsters the art of memorizing scripture nowadays, but memorized scripture can be an enormously valuable source of spiritual sustenance across a lifetime, particularly in crisis. Families can help children learn portions of the Bible by heart, both by encouraging individual memorization of selected texts and by reciting certain passages together in family worship. Psalms of thanks and praise lend themselves particularly well to such practices. Psalm verses or short psalms can be used as meal graces easily committed to memory, some-times through song. Those psalms traditionally assigned by the church to Night Prayer have a comforting effect and could be used with children in bedtime rituals if the family does not ob-serve a practice of Night Prayer together.

## Using Imagination and Role Play with Scripture

We have noted the ease with which children engage in imagina-tive prayer. Imagination is a marvelous tool to use in unearthing the vitality and drama of scripture as well. It is especially appro-priate for use with narrative portions of scripture, where often colorful characters populate the story and the dynamics of hu-man interaction are full of feelings that elicit natural response. When a passage is read during family worship, parents can ask questions aimed at stimulating an imaginative encounter with the text: What do you think it was like to be Joseph, thrown into the well by his brothers? How do you think his brothers felt toward Joseph, and why? Or, what would it be like to be paralyzed? How would you feel if you were completely dependent on oth-ers? It is often a revealing exercise to ask family members to imagine what it might be like to stand in the shoes of each char-acter in a biblical story.

Children love acting too and often learn more from a story by entering into its drama than by hearing about it. It is fun as well as instructive for families to act out together some of the stories they read. This makes worship playful and enjoyable, an important ingredient especially for young children but pertinent even to adults. The context need not be worship in any formal sense. Why wouldn't a skit based on some scripture story or par-able make a good rainy-day activity? The children could work it out and put it on for their parents. Or the entire family could play biblical charades, guessing which story or character was being portrayed in mime by various members.

Let me suggest again that if the congregation is the only context in which scripture is dealt with, the artificial dichotomy between faith and life is perpetuated and reinforced. Children quickly perceive that the church is for "sacred" activities and the home for "secular" ones.

All the practices described thus far help in the gradual process of making God's Word our home. The foundation and cornerstone of this home have already been laid for us in Jesus Christ. We have the privileged task of building a temple for the living God, not only in our bodies but in our relationships. As we offer to God the discipline of becoming acquainted with scripture, we need to remember that "unless the Lord builds the house, those who build it labor in vain" (Psalm 127:1). God's grace works through our practices to build a temple fit for divine worship.

## Ancestral Stories

As families take time to discuss, imagine, or act out Bible readings, they gradually make connections between the stories of scripture and their own life stories. Then another level of family storytelling enriches the process, the level of ancestral identity and history. Not only parents but extended family members, especially grandparents, have a special role to play in passing on to new generations a clear sense of their lineage and heritage. It is not primarily the biological link that is critical here but the values, dreams, and motives of earlier generations—the choices that have shaped in fundamental ways who *this* family is now.

Previous generations have traditionally seen their lives as deeply rooted in faith and have had years to consider specific life events and movements in light of that faith. The faith-filled interpretations of life experience that come from parents, grandparents, and a wider circle of relations can be both enormously revealing and supportive to newer generations.

Earlier we noted that grandmothers have an especially esteemed role in the experience of many black families. Both Martin Luther King, Jr., and Howard Thurman—two of the most respected African American Christians in our nation's history—were deeply influenced by the love and faith of their grandmothers. The impact of grandparents on children's faith formation seems a virtually universal phenomenon. Author Ernest Boyer recounts the impact of two grandparents on his family's experience of faith. Boyer's grandfather had a magnificent capacity to be fully present to him as a child, a gift of personal affirmation that Boyer now understands as one of the most important ministries family members can provide to one another. He knew his grandfather as one who saw God in every person. The Italian immigrant grandmother of Boyer's wife had an extraordinary ability to give herself to her family and to others in joyful and unself-conscious sacrifice. This grandmother spent a lifetime engaged in what Boyer calls "the sacrament of the care of others."[6]

Many of us have been deeply affected by the evidences of faith we have seen in our parents or other significant family adults. Something immediate and real emerges about the life stories from our own family history. The ways a parent responds in faith to the loss of a spouse or a child, to a divorce, to a serious or chronic illness, to a truly wonderful or unexpected grace, to the tragic or miraculous events of life in the larger world—these create indelible impressions on children whose spirits are being formed in the web of family interaction as surely as are their psyches.

Basic postures toward life, such as trust or fear, are communicated indirectly to children by adults, quite apart from the beliefs, doctrines, and morals adults may teach. Whether a child gradually becomes open and trusting or anxious and defensive in disposition has serious implications for the Christian spiritual life. In this respect we see that spiritual formation involves far more than what has typically been meant by catechesis or Christian education. It becomes increasingly clear how central the role of significant adults within the home is to this kind of formation.

## Family Adults as Spiritual Guides

Those of our parents and grandparents who have acted as early tutors and embodiments of faith have been, in fact, our first spiritual guides. Sometimes another relative, family friend, or pastor has acted in this capacity. The tradition of godparents speaks to the wisdom that parents cannot be all things to their own children and that friends of faith beyond the immediate family may be better able to encourage a child's spiritual growth at certain points along the way. Still, it is a loss to the whole family if parents cannot play a central role as beacons of hope and models of faith.

Spiritual guidance is a many-colored coat. At times the guide is primarily a model or exemplar, still the most profound and effective form of teaching. At times the guide needs to engage in explicit teaching, perhaps to clarify misperceptions. Helping people put words to their experience is a fundamental aspect of guidance. But the essential task is best described as that of *midwifery*.[7] Because the spirit of God is mysteriously at work within each person, the real work of guidance is simply to recognize and enable the work that God is doing already. The guide aids in bringing to birth a whole person, which is God's great labor of love. Human beings can be instruments that either facilitate or block this spiritual birth.

Many dimensions of parenting have this midwifing character. Yet sometimes a grandparent or other adult one step removed from the daily stresses of parenting, is less likely to get in the way of God's labor. The challenge is to respond to the child's most urgent plea, as Cavalletti hears it: "Help me to come closer to God by myself." Another way to put this is, "Help me to know and name my own experience of God."

My friend whose family shares the upcoming day in morning prayer is fond of pointing out that Christian education is all too often about other people's experiences of faith at the expense of helping us recognize and articulate our own experience. When a child asks you a question about God, it is not an abstract question; it is a question about how *you* know and experience God. One of the most helpful things we as parents and adult mentors can do is to put words to our own experience of God and allow the child to make connections with his or her experience.

It is essential for adults in the home as well as in the congregation to understand that children have their own spiritual experiences and perceptions, their own unique inner mystery that belongs to God alone. Children are neither blank screens on which adults may write their scripts nor empty vessels that adults are duty-bound to fill up with doctrines and moral regulations.

Children arrive in this world with definite personalities; with motives, dreams, and drives to which adults can never be fully privy. Yet they are malleable to adult nurture and teaching in a host of ways, especially in the early years of life.

Children need their spiritual dimension affirmed and supported; they need firm but loving discipline to give secure parameters to their growth; and they need adults to point faithfully to God with trust and joy. To the extent that parents, grandparents, and other adults of faith fulfill these basic needs, they provide spiritual guidance for the younger generation. Weaving together stories of scripture, family history, and personal experience is a fundamental aspect of such guidance.

## Seeking God's Guidance Together

One of the more neglected ways in which adults can provide guidance in the home is by teaching mutual discernment and consensus decision making. Discernment is a process of seeking guidance from God concerning what is true, good, or divinely willed in an ambiguous situation. Life is full of "wheat and tares" growing together, so much so that it is often hard to distinguish between what is healthy food and what looks good but cannot yield nourishment. Discernment becomes important to people of faith when a key decision needs to be made, and conflicting feelings arise about the relative merits of each choice. Therefore the way decisions are made can be closely related to the process of discernment, although persons seldom consider spiritual discernment as a prerequisite for most common decisions.

In many situations, especially early in a child's life, discernment and decision making belong, of necessity, to parents. But as children grow older, their capacity to make choices in appropriate spheres needs to be recognized and encouraged. The more children are included in family decision making, the more ownership and harmony there will be among family members.

Many families have a family council process of one sort or another. In some homes, councils are called only for the most serious problems; in other households, family councils are a weekly or monthly institution convened regardless of whether or not a particular issue has arisen. Generally the purpose of such meetings is to air grievances, discuss family rules or practices, make creative suggestions, and find out what other members are thinking or feeling. Often an issue will surface from regular meetings that can be addressed before it becomes a major problem.

A marvelous way to develop the family's capacity for co-operation is to practice consensus decision making. Quakers have a long history with this corporate discipline from which others of us could learn much. Consensus stipulates that no decision is reached until all members have arrived at the same course of action in their own conscience. This alternative to conventional majority-vote decision making has serious spiritual implications. For one, it presumes the presence and action of the Holy Spirit in the midst of the gathered members, and it presumes that the Spirit has a will to communicate through the faithful. What is needed, then, is for those present to place their own desires and presuppositions aside in order to listen for the whisperings of the divine will within the heart. "That of God in every person" is trusted to reveal the light of insight to each individual who seeks it with genuine openness, and the consensus reached is understood to confirm the will of God in the matter.

It should be clear from this description that the classical practice of consensus is more a process of spiritual discernment than of decision making in any common sense. The decision belongs to God, and we are simply channels through which that decision becomes clarified. This manner of approaching needed decisions in a community obviously requires more time than a majority vote. To discern what the Spirit is leading one toward asks for contemplative space—a setting and time that invite deep and prayerful reflection, even if in the midst of routine activity.

While designed for larger faith communities and assuming a reasonably mature faith generally found in adults, such a practice can be usefully adapted to family life. When an important decision needs to be made, family members can meet in council to discuss various options, listing pros and cons for each alternative. Pros and cons would include both factual and emotional data. Each person then takes the possibilities into a time of prayerful reflection. During this individual stage of discernment, the first effort is to let go of personal preferences in order to hear what God might be communicating for the good of the family as a whole.

The second discipline is to sort out which factors carry more weight. Option number one may have five pros and two cons, but the cons have more far-reaching consequences than the pros; option number two may have eight pros, but half of them seem rather frivolous in light of our Christian calling. This stage of the process may need several days or even weeks, depending on the magnitude of the decision. Scriptural reflection and prayer within the family during this time can play a significant role in the discernment process. When everyone feels led to a particular choice, the council meets again to hear how each member has felt moved and what reasoning has arisen from personal reflection. If consensus does not emerge, more information and expressions of feeling are offered for consideration and the discernment process continues.

Of course, sometimes deadlines determine when a decision must be reached. Even if the process can't take its full and natural course, a time of prayerful discernment for each family member can prove valuable. In these cases, a more conventional method of decision making may need to be combined with an abbreviated discernment time, where differences of direction are settled by majority choice. In such instances, however, it is important to acknowledge that the use of majority opinion is a compromise solution and may not reflect the wisdom of the Holy Spirit. The felt leadings of family members in the minority need to be affirmed and differences accepted as such.

Moreover, a continuing process of discernment after making a decision tests the choice in light of circumstances and inner perceptions that follow. How well does the decision hold up over time? Does it continue to seem right to those who elected it initially? Have those with differing perspectives come to see it as the fitting choice or have their reservations grown deeper? Sometimes a family may want to change its decision based on the process of continued discernment.

Obviously decisions can be made (and most often are) without a spiritual discernment component. Families can gather simply to discuss alternatives, weigh relative advantages, and come to an agreement out of good listening and interpersonal communication. How to spend the weekend, where to go on vacation, how to deal with a stubborn quarrel in the family—these are generally matters for simple family councils. Major decisions require discernment: a change in vocation, whether or not to accept a new job that entails moving, how to deal creatively with problematic friends or relatives where the interaction is clearly recognized as a problem by the family.[8] Some matters—for example, how to allocate available family resources among charitable or other significant causes—will carry more weight for one family than another and therefore determine whether or not they are subject to in-depth discernment.

Parents will need to exercise discretion about which issues call simply for discussion and which ones require a more reflective process. Some kinds of discernment are appropriate for the whole family, others for parents or parents and older children. However, I would hesitate to underestimate the capabilities of younger children. If they are given a chance to think about clear alternatives, perhaps to hear an appropriate biblical story and to play with related symbols, we might be genuinely surprised at the intuitions of younger children. Spiritual discernment is a vital process for children to learn, as it can help them make personal decisions throughout life. To use it in the family context also teaches that genuine discernment is a mutual process requiring a community of faith for confirmation.

The process of discernment clearly takes time—unhurried, reflective, open-ended time. Authentic discernment involves a distinct element of letting go and resting. The process is, at heart, one of allowing God's desire to surface from deep within, to percolate up through all our typical distractions. Such restful time is an excellent description of Sabbath. Family discernment needs Sabbath time—time set apart from the frenetic activity of work, school, meetings, afterschool athletics, and lessons. The Sabbath is time emptied of self-preoccupied and self-important agendas, time given back to God for God's purposes.

Contemporary biblical scholar Walter Brueggemann argues rather convincingly that "the sabbath commandment functions as the center and interpretive focus for the entire decalogue."[9] The Sabbath is an affirmation that God's sovereignty and governance are to be trusted absolutely. After all, God is so secure about the order and goodness of creation that God can rest; and if God can rest, who are we to try to improve on God's example? To keep the Sabbath is to participate in God's own rest, a radical response of trust in the power of the Spirit to uphold creation.

In our fast-track, power-minded culture that is intent on ceaseless achievement, productivity, problem-solving, and success (a mentality all too many families and churches are caught up in), keeping the Sabbath is a way of reclaiming God and relinquishing our idols. Sabbath is the desperately needed contemplative dimension of life, which has been so disastrously missing from a rationalistic and domineering Western culture for centuries. Only from the quiet center of listening to God and discerning God's call does our genuine productivity and service to others emerge. Service is, quite naturally then, the topic of our next chapter.

## *For Reflection*

～How did your family convey the good news story to you when you were growing up? Does your family use scripture at home now? If so, how? What new approaches would you like to try?

～Who are (or were) the ancestral storytellers in your family? What key figures in your family background have had an impact on your experience of faith?

～Which adults were spiritual guides for you in your early formation? How might you provide guidance in your household now?

～Which models of seeking God's guidance as a family attracted your attention in this chapter?

# 8

# The Family
# as Servant

~

*You call me Teacher and Lord—and you are right, for that is what I am. So if I, your Lord and Teacher, have washed your feet, you also ought to wash one another's feet.*
—John 13:13-14

WE BEGAN OUR DISCUSSION OF FAMILIES as sacred shelters by suggesting that a genuine sacred shelter "releases its members for the pastoral care of the world." It is time to consider how, through the spiritual nurture and training of the home, family members are supported to engage in the mission to which all Christians are called.

I will stress from the start that prayer and scriptural reflection are in no way opposed to active service. There is a strong tendency in our churches and in society at large to view interior spiritual disciplines as somehow antithetical to active service. The stereotype pits withdrawn, "contemplative" types against the tireless, dedicated servers of the world. These polarizations reveal the extent to which neither Christian prayer nor Christian service is adequately understood in our culture. When both are authentic, it becomes abundantly clear how inseparable they are. We might recall that the same Luther who said, "I cannot get on without spending three hours daily in prayer" was one of the most prodigiously energetic and productive servants in the history of the church.

Within the framework of faith, the only service of genuine and lasting value is undergirded by prayer. If our desire to serve is not taken into the crucible of prayer to be tested by the flame of God's truth, even our best human motives can hide subtle forms of self-serving. Sometimes we serve in order to win praise or gain attention; sometimes our service is imprinted with a martyr complex, designed to garner the sympathy of others; sometimes our service is an expression of perfectionist compulsions rather than a free offering of self. In a reversal of ordinary perspective on what constitutes social service, eminent Quaker writer Douglas Steere calls intercessory prayer "the most intensely social act that the human being is capable of," precisely because when done in secret "it is mercifully preserved from . . . the possible corruptions to which all outer deeds of service for others are subject."[1]

Prayer does more than purify our motives for ministry, however; it offers God an ear open to the whisperings of the divine will. Prayer leads us into the compassionate heart of God. Indeed, if prayer does not reveal to us the whole creation residing in God's providential love and care, we should suspect illusion; and if we do not find ourselves bidden to participate in the divine embrace of all creatures, we may be sure that sin is distorting our practice of prayer. Someone on retreat once commented, "We can't adore and ignore." Adoration of God is a chimera if it leads us to ignore a world God loved enough to send Jesus to die for.

Regular meditation on the full range of scripture will help preserve prayer from becoming self-absorbed. It is virtually impossible to hear the prophets' call for social righteousness, to reflect on Jesus' ministry to the sick and despised, or to absorb his teachings on what makes for blessed living without comprehending that we are called to minister in the same spirit. Families who are faithful in disciplines of prayer and scriptural reflection will find themselves drawn to acts of service and mission by their Lord.

We have already discussed the ministry that family members can provide to one another and the critical nature of this mutual care. The capacity to love and serve begins in the laboratory of home life. But if family life is to escape becoming an idol, such ministry must extend beyond the boundaries of the family circle and beyond the larger circumference of familiar friends and communities.

How does a family foster this response to the wider world? Gwen White, a leader and teacher in the spirituality of the family, identifies several arenas in which attitudes of service and mission can be nurtured within family life.[2] I have chosen to focus on three that seem especially pertinent: the ministry of stewardship, the ministry of acceptance, and the ministry of outreach.

## The Ministry of Stewardship

Stewardship involves our attitude toward and treatment of *all* our resources. One of the most precious resources available to us is the earth itself. Families of faith can make an enormous contribution to the ailing health of our planet by showing genuine concern for the earth, which is habitat to all living things, including ourselves. Children can be taught to respect and value other life-forms and to understand that our lives and theirs are inextricably bound together.

Families can engage in valuing the creatures of this earth in innumerable ways. Feeding birds and creating or preserving natural nesting sites in the yard are simple and enjoyable family activities. Teaching children which creatures pose a real threat to human beings and which do not means less indiscriminate harm to wildlife. Planting grass on eroded soil and learning to compost for gardening are good practices of family stewardship. Families also would do well to educate themselves about alternatives to many common household and garden products that contain toxic chemicals with long-term adverse consequences for soil, water, and living creatures.

Some excellent television programs educate families on the beauties of our natural heritage and convey constructive ways of maintaining the delicate and necessary balances of the natural world. Families might also consider supporting an organization dedicated to the preservation of wild creatures and their habitats.

The way families treat their material resources is closely tied to concern for the earth and its inhabitants. Families of faith will want to resist the voracious machine of consumerism, which grows more menacing every year. The more we "buy into" our seemingly inexhaustible supply of consumer products, the more we tip the balance of economic distribution toward the affluent and away from the poor. Additionally, the more we consume, the more waste we produce in the form of excessive packaging, broken gadgets, and clothing that is out of fashion in six months. Waste is rapidly becoming a major environmental crisis worldwide. After nearly twenty years of neglect, the renewed national interest in recycling can serve as an impetus to families to recycle all the waste they can, as well as to support the development and expansion of community recycling programs. However recycling waste is no substitute for producing less waste.

Both as a matter of environmental concern and as a matter of global economic justice, consumerism in the United States is a moral issue for families of faith to consider in all seriousness. Family spirituality cannot be separated from simplicity of lifestyle. One of the most important spiritual disciplines in family life today, especially in the affluent West, is the intentional nurture of nonmaterialistic values in an increasingly materialistic world.

Attitudes and practices with regard to money become a significant dimension of family spirituality when viewed as a form of responsible stewardship. As children grow older, it is a healthy practice for families to consider together the use of financial resources. Decisions may need to be made about what purchases are really necessary and what criteria will determine which nonessentials are in keeping with a life of faithfulness to God. Various good causes will compete for contributions in a family where social and environmental needs are taken to heart. How will its members make choices about what to support? Family councils and consensus decision making may be especially useful here.

The practice of tithing or at least pledging some portion of personal money for a larger good needs to be encouraged from the time children are young. Children can learn to offer a percentage of their allowances to the church. They also can be encouraged to join with other family members in various fundraising projects for special offerings or favored causes. Bake sales, garage sales, or neighborhood car washes are some of the activities families might enjoy, as a family unit or together with other church or neighborhood families.

Adults can encourage children to develop their natural generosity in other ways. In some cultures, if a child admires a toy belonging to another child, the owner will simply give the admirer the toy. Would that we could find ways of modeling and affirming such generosity in our overly possessive culture!

Many of the activities suggested for families during a season like Lent lend themselves to the practice of charity and simplicity. Gertrud Mueller Nelson's description of the "alms box" her family uses during Lent is a fitting example. (See chapter 6.) Not only is the giving an act of care, but the simplified living that underlies it is a small redress of the imbalance of the resources in our society. It is important that parents interpret such practices as a matter of justice as well as a matter of charity.

## The Ministry of Acceptance

Earlier we described how crucial the practice of personal acceptance is to spiritual growth within family life. If acceptance of differences is adequately nurtured among family members, it is a natural step to extend the same kind of acceptance to those beyond family parameters. Prejudice, ignorance, and fear still riddle our society when it comes to persons we consider "different" from ourselves. Parents need to make an effort to become aware of their own biases and work actively at overcoming them. They can, through example and teaching, help their children be open to all kinds of people.

Every dimension of home life reflects certain values. The books and magazines that are read, the TV programs watched, the friends families cultivate, the schools children attend, the neighborhoods families live in, and the churches they elect to join—all these have an enormously formative impact on children's attitudes toward those perceived as different from themselves. Parents will want to exercise great care in such choices, where choice is available, in order to encourage healthy attitudes toward persons of different races, religions, cultures, economic circumstances, and physical and mental capacity.

Most mainline churches are making a concerted effort to celebrate diversity rather than ignore, suppress, or deny it. Church families would do well to join the effort by modeling and encouraging attitudes of acceptance both within and beyond the home. The basic respect with which adults think and speak about different kinds of people will exert a positive influence on children's attitudes; but, as always, the most effective way to shape the behavior of future generations is to model genuinely caring personal interaction. If parents feel awkward or uncomfortable with certain kinds of people, it is best to be open about those feelings with children, who will likely be well aware of the discomfort no matter how parents try to hide it. There is no harm in adults' admitting that they are still working to overcome stereotypes inherited or absorbed from the culture. Sometimes our children are the ones who help us become more open and accepting.

## The Ministry of Outreach

The two arenas of family service just considered have dealt primarily with attitude development as it affects response to the wider world. Habits of global thinking, patterns of stewardship, and attitudes of acceptance *can* be expressed largely within the home environment. However, the third arena, outreach, moves families directly into the community at large; a ministry of outreach cannot be housebound. Whether working at a local soup kitchen, assuming volunteer duties in a shelter for the homeless, or joining a walk for the hungry, through outreach the family is participating more visibly in the social witness and mission of the church.

James and Kathleen McGinnis, founders of the National Parenting for Peace and Justice Network in St. Louis, Missouri, point out that many Christian families in the United States see the larger society principally as a threat to their cherished "family values." Values such as intimacy, affection, support, communication, responsibility, mutual trust, and fidelity can be fully affirmed by the church since they are values shared by the community of faith. The problem comes when families believe the only way to realize such values is to retreat from society into the cocoon of the home. An irony here parallels the truth that no person can be a Christian by withdrawing into a private relationship with God. The Christian realizes spiritual identity only in relation to God *and* neighbor, as the Great Commandment stresses. Jesus makes it abundantly, if uncomfortably, clear in the parable of the good Samaritan (Luke 10:29-37) that the "neighbor" of the Gospel is precisely the one we would prefer to despise, ignore, or shun. Likewise, the family cannot realize its full potential as family by itself; that occurs only in relation to society as a whole—a society whose ills it often would rather deplore or ignore.

Leckey reminds us that "outreach is as essential to the identity of the Christian family as prayer and worship. Often, in fact, it is through the social outreach and mission dimension that the interior life of a person or a family group grows and deepens."[3] The McGinnises reinforce her point: "Family values are realized not only by 'spending more time with the family' but also by participating as a family and with other families in the transformation of the world. . . . Family community is built in part by participation in the building of neighborhood and global community."[4]

Families need the community of other faithful families to overcome natural resistance to engaging in social concerns. The resistance comes from many sources: fear of involvement, time and energy constraints, discouragement at the overwhelming nature of many social problems, and feelings of being ill-equipped and poorly informed. Individual families need the encouragement, equipping, and inspiration that come from the larger church and from other committed families within it.

## Levels of Participation in Mission

The McGinnises suggest three levels at which families can participate in the church's social mission.[5] The first is lifestyle changes within the home that embody the values of faith over the values of the culture. We have discussed these in some measure. Dolores Leckey identifies six values in family life that counter the dominant values of our culture:

∼being, as opposed to doing / producing / achieving;

∼sharing, as opposed to possessing;

∼creating, as opposed to consuming;

∼self-worth, as opposed to status / privilege;

∼mercy / reconciliation, as opposed to rigid justice / revenge;

∼equality, as opposed to domination / subordination.[6]

Families who have learned to embody countercultural values are in a position to witness prophetically not only to the culture but also to the larger church, which has at times showed itself more captive to dominant cultural values than some of its member families.

The second level of family participation in the church's social mission is what the McGinnises call "works of mercy." These are responses to the needs of people who have been victimized by physical or social ills. Volunteering to help at battered women's shelters, substance abuse hotlines, day-care centers, or transportation and meal services for the elderly represents this kind of ministry. Walkathons for the hungry and other fundraisers for charity are also examples of this second level of participation in mission.

The third level—"works of justice"—is no doubt the most demanding. These aim to challenge unfair and destructive values in the institutions and laws of our society and to help envision and create alternative structures. Writing letters to congressional representatives or others in positions of decision-making power; joining support rallies or protest marches to voice positions; devising and submitting alternative policy platforms; even engaging in acts of civil disobedience if the means of changing unjust policies in a democratic society fail and conscience so dictates—

all such responses qualify for this third level of participation in the church's social mission.

Most Christian families have no difficulty in principle with the first two levels of participation in social witness. The third level can be problematic for those who believe that political and spiritual spheres of life are somehow incompatible and not to be joined. Some believe that God calls us not to transform the world but only to be transformed personally. Here again, knowledge of scripture, tradition, and basic church history is extremely important. The witness of scripture alone would indicate that God has called for changes in the social order among people of faith for millennia:

> Is not this the sort of fast that pleases me
> —it is the Lord Yahweh who speaks—
> to break unjust fetters
> and undo the thongs of the yoke,
> to let the oppressed go free,
> and break every yoke,
> to share your bread with the hungry,
> and shelter the homeless poor . . . ?
> —Isaiah 58:6-7, JB

While sharing bread with the hungry and sheltering the homeless poor fit the "works of mercy" category, breaking unjust fetters and letting the oppressed go free require change in the unjust structures of the world.

The Reformed tradition has historically understood Christian vocation in the world to include "work for the transformation of cultural, political and economic institutions—consistent with the vision and values of God's commonwealth."[7] The Roman Catholic church, often historically allied with the powers of state government, has produced a number of remarkable documents since Vatican II, some directly encouraging families to engage in world-transforming tasks:

> The family must also see to it that the virtues of which it is the teacher and guardian should be enshrined in laws and institutions. It is of the highest importance that families should together devote themselves directly and by common

agreement to transforming the very structure of society. Otherwise, families will become the first victims of the evils that they will have watched idly and with indifference.[8]

## Making Choices

Because families in today's society are beleaguered and the pressures for engagement intense, they must learn to set priorities and make choices in every area of intentional discipline. Family service to the wider community is often the last to receive attention, simply because parental energy is more than expended in the internal maintenance of family life and daily business. (How often the same dynamic is at work in the life of congregations, whose energies are depleted by internal maintenance so that little is left for mission in the world!)

As with all aspects of family spiritual practice, choices will need to be made about how the household witnesses to its faith. Certain forms of service are more appropriate while children are young, and others make better sense as children mature. The whole family need not be engaged in every activity chosen, as there may be differences in what family members feel called to and varying levels of commitment even within a commonly perceived call. A single member can represent the whole family as long as the family supports that individual's ministry.

It is a matter of critical discernment on the part of parents, especially when children are young, to determine whether levels of personal engagement in a cause prove beneficial or detrimental to the family as a whole. A dear friend of mine who became deeply involved in peace work realized after a few years that the intensity of her engagement with the cause—a cause extremely relevant to her children's futures—was interfering with the character of her relationship with those children. She had become highly anxious, attaching more weight to the success of the peace group than it could reasonably bear and feeling herself indispensable to its effectiveness. The level of stress was affecting her health and the health of her whole family. My friend wisely decided to reduce the level of her engagement with the cause.

When the time adults give to worthy service organizations denies their children adequate parental nurture, priorities need reexamining. Children should not be forced to pay the price of their parents' commitments if it means robbing them of necessary relational foundations for healthy emotional development. When parents bring children into the world, they tacitly accept responsibility to provide those children with the stability of a loving, secure, and trustworthy home environment, an environment that has far more to do with the quality of parental presence than with material security.

It helps to remember that all forms of family spiritual nurture act to shape mature persons who can function creatively within society at large. If overt and visible forms of outreach cannot be reasonably handled in the family at particular times, it does not mean that family life is shorn of its opportunities to express service to God. A whole and healthy family *is* a service to this world, and the pastoral care that family members provide one another is the *principal* ministry of family life, preceding and undergirding all other forms of ministry.

These are simple and natural ways in which the family, out of its own identity, ministers to others. Hospitality, as previously observed, is a form of outreach inside the home. Douglas Steere reminded us that intercessory prayer constitutes a form of outreach more profound than many of us realize. Evelyn Underhill's insight seems especially pertinent in this regard: "We are not separate, ring-fenced spirits. We penetrate each other, influence each other for good and evil, for the giving or taking of vitality, all the time. . . . The value and reality of our souls is at least as much social as individual."[9] If who we are as individuals is already a social reality, the identity of families magnifies this truth.

The point is simply that families are not ends in and of themselves. They are woven into the fabric of society. Church families are knit together in the body of Christ as well. They are blessed instruments of growth, called to channel divine grace through their unique pattern of relationships: "The particularity of conjugal and familial love is a means by which the spouses aid each other and their children to live lives of universal love and social responsibility."[10]

## *For Reflection*

～In what ways do you find prayer, scripture, and service related?

～What forms of stewardship can you envision practicing within your home?

～How does your family express acceptance of persons who are different?

～What kinds of outreach seem feasible in family life? What seems problematic? Why?

# 9

# Gathered Church, Domestic Church

~

*For I have come to set a man against his father, and a daughter against her mother, and a daughter-in-law against her mother-in-law; and one's foes will be those of one's own household. Whoever loves father or mother more than me is not worthy of me; and whoever loves son or daughter more than me is not worthy of me.*

—Matthew 10:35-37

WE HAVE CONSIDERED SOME of the key ways in which the family lives out its calling to be a sacred shelter for the sake of the world God loves. It is time to return to our central thesis that the family is the primary locus of spiritual formation and to root it more securely in the soil of Christian theology.

## The Problem

There is a sharply felt tension about the value of the family in New Testament teachings, a tension largely absent from the Old Testament. In Hebrew culture, marriage was expected, and children were celebrated as gifts from God. A woman's barrenness was considered a social disgrace and a sign of God's disfavor. As we have noted, the spiritual traditions of Jewish life were celebrated regularly in the home where father and mother exercised a priestly role within the family Sabbath ritual. Jesus, on the other hand, had some radically disturbing things to say about the place of natural kinship, as the above passage from Matthew's Gospel reveals.

Celibate expressions of Christian discipleship emerged forcefully in the early centuries of church growth, largely a response to the imminent expectation of Jesus' return and the consummation of the kingdom of God. The eremitic and monastic movements developed in response to the official "Christianization" of civilization under Constantine, wherein the radical nature of Christian discipleship was perceived to have been diluted. Both Orthodox and Roman Catholic traditions cultivated monastic expressions of Christian life. In the Western church, priesthood was joined to celibacy; in the Orthodox East, priests were allowed to marry.

Consequently, the tensions surrounding marriage and family issues have been felt more keenly in the Roman Catholic church, where becoming a priest, monk, or nun has historically been elevated as a spiritually superior choice in life. What Boyer terms "the spirituality of life at the edge"—the practice of celibacy, poverty, and obedience—has often been treated as the single genuine context for Christian sanctification. Therefore, despite several excellent theological statements on the value of the family within their tradition, some Roman Catholics experience the church as denying that the family is a valid context for growth in sanctity.

The Reformers fully intended to reclaim congregational life as the center of Christian piety in place of the corrupt monastic institutions of medieval Europe. In keeping with their focus on the laity, the Reformers labored to revive the dignity of families, urging them to practice piety within the home as well as to join in congregational worship regularly. Access to scripture in the common language was a sixteenth-century revolution. It is not hard to envision how, in such a context, families of faith might begin to see themselves as transmitters of sacred tradition, colaborers in the church's ministry rather than profane recipients of the church's absolution.

Despite the implications of the Reformation for family life in the church, the heirs of Luther, Calvin, and Zwingli are often just as perplexed about the place of families in Christianity as their Roman Catholic counterparts. Ernest Boyer recounts the story of a woman lawyer, highly active in her Protestant congregation, who decided to take time out from her busy career to care for two small children. Despite initial fears of feeling confined and aimless, she soon found herself more fulfilled in parenting than she could ever have imagined. Her efforts to integrate her parental role with her *faith*, however, met with unanticipated barriers. Finally, in great frustration, she went to see her minister. "I'm finished; I'm never going to read the New Testament again!" she declared vehemently. Her minister, greatly surprised, asked why. "Because Jesus does not seem to have a single good thing to say about families. He says that a person who follows him must leave his wife, children, and parents. He says that this person must also give away all he owns—can I really raise my children like that? . . . Where do I fit in?"[1]

## New Testament Perspectives on the Family

There can be no doubt that Jesus relativized the importance of the family, not only in his teachings but in his own "single" lifestyle. The call to follow Jesus was a radical one; his disciples left all in order to follow him (Mark 10:28), although Peter and others apparently still had wives and most likely had children given the assumptions of the culture. Paul's encouragement toward the celibate life and his explicit valuing of this state over marriage have reinforced the church's tendency to look upon family life as a second-class expression of Christian faith.

On the other hand, the New Testament writings are replete with family images, terms, and illustrations. Jesus uses the familiar name "Abba" (the Aramaic equivalent of "Daddy") to address God. His direct naming of God with such an intimate family term strongly suggests a familial dynamic at the heart of the Holy Trinity. Jesus blesses the marriage feast at Cana with wine, a symbol of abundant goodness and joy (John 2:1-11), and he expresses a very high view of the nature of marriage (Mark 10:6-9). He blesses little children and identifies their childlike qualities as the gateway to the kingdom of heaven (Mark 10:13-16), and he describes God's unconditional love in the homespun figures of a father with his profligate son (Luke 15:11-32). All these suggest a higher valuing of the family than might be apparent from a surface reading of some of Jesus' "hard" teachings.

Jesus' perspective on the family of kinship is perhaps most clearly revealed in Mark 3:31-35, where his mother and brothers arrive to speak with him while he is teaching a crowd. On being told that his family seeks him, he asks, "Who are my mother and my brothers?" Then looking around to those listening to him, he answers his own query: "Whoever does the will of God is my brother and sister and mother." In a single sentence, Jesus has redefined the family from core to periphery: A true family is one whose center is unswerving allegiance to God alone and whose parameters expand to include everyone who delights in God's will. Jesus is interested in inaugurating a new community. Yet even this community of grace is described in family terms, *oikeios*, the "household" of God (Eph. 2:19). What does the use of such familial images reveal?

## Theological Considerations

Sang H. Lee, seeking a Reformed theological understanding of the family, follows Jonathan Edward's vision by suggesting that the human family is a "type" of God's self-giving love within the created order. Although sinful and in need of redemption, the family still reveals something profound of the beauty and fidelity of divine love. The priority of the kingdom of God does not *de*value but *re*values the family in light of a larger truth. Jesus relativizes natural family ties in relation to the kingdom, where the institution of marriage will not be needed (see Mark 12:25); yet in so doing he does not abolish the importance of the kinship family but indicates the context in which it receives its true vocation. In Sang's view, the kinship family fulfills its genuine potential as a "type" of God's sacrificial love only to the extent that it embodies the priorities of the kingdom and the values of the new community.[2]

If we fail to establish clearly the transvalued place of the family in Christian theology, we will succumb to our cultural habit of idolizing the family. When we sentimentalize or idealize any community, we make an idol of it: "By idealizing community, we invest in it those trusts and loyalties which belong to God alone."[3] Unfortunately, as our social fabric tears and traditional structures crumble, increasingly wide segments of our religious culture resort to sentimentality and idealization with respect to the family. There is a strong strain of isolationism in the popular phrase "Your home is your castle," as if families could be insulated from a culture permeating their own structure. It is inconceivable to treat the family as an insular unit, just as it is impossible to isolate an individual from the matrix of relationships shaping his or her individuality. As I have tried to indicate, if the family becomes merely a fortress against the inhumanity of the world, it will be incapable of serving a creative and redemptive role in that world.

The kinship family is viewed primarily as a biological and sociological entity. Within the church, however, the family becomes more than the most efficient unit for human propagation, nurture, and ordering of society. It becomes part of the larger, transforming kinship of those bound together in baptism to the body of Christ. Everything said thus far about the Christian spiritual life of the family has its source and origin in the life, mission, and ministry of the church of Jesus Christ.

The church is the context for our entire discussion of family spirituality. Without this context we will indeed reinforce cultural idolatry of the nuclear family. Yet we tend to restrict our vision of "church" either to the place of weekly worship or to the programmatic activities of a particular congregation. The church universal is constituted of the whole company of saints: those who have gone before us, those present in every part of this world, and those who will come after us. Remarkably, Jesus has promised that where even two or three are gathered in his name, he is present in their midst (Matt. 18:20). The body of Christ is realized wherever Christians gather to celebrate his risen presence and live out his mission by the power of the Holy Spirit. Therefore the church is gathered in more ways and places than those commonly represented in weekly liturgy and congregational life.

The Christian family, even in its most basic unit of couple, is an expression of the church. Like any congregation, the family is a partial gathering of the body; yet each joining of Christians is, at least potentially, a real expression of the reconciling, unifying love of Christ. In the Eastern church, Orthodox priests bless the homes of their members as a sacramental sign that wherever Christians dwell they sanctify space. The homes of holy people are holy places. Thus the kinship family is taken into the embrace of God's spiritual family and transfigured into a particular embodiment of the communion of saints. The center and boundary is Christ alone. Yet within this greater truth, the believing family, like the congregation of which it is a part, is revealed to be a blessed community for learning and living a pattern of kingdom relationships.

The question underlying all our reflection has been that of *where* the vision and values of the church get communicated and lived out most effectively. Our thesis has been that families are central not only to human formation but to Christian formation. The persistence in New Testament writings of family metaphors for the kingdom of God reveals the quintessentially relational character of our faith. Our relationship with God is the core of the spiritual life, the ground and compass for all other relationships. Yet our relationships with others are the measure and reflection of the reality of our relationship with God.

The Christian life is unavoidably relational. Sociologically, families are the primary nexus of relationships in which we learn how to live with one another. Like all intentional communities, families are intensive crucibles of relationship. Therefore relationships within the Christian family are not merely *figures* of spiritual relationships but *vehicles* through which we may begin to live out the new creation in Christ.

In speaking of family as the primary center of spiritual formation, I have had in mind two specific meanings. First, sociologically and psychodynamically, any family has a critical formative impact for good or ill on its members that reflects a basic spiritual reality. Second, the family of committed faith, comprised of individual members of the church, can be the most consistent arena of Christian formation for its members if it so chooses. Theologically speaking, the church is the primary place of our spiritual formation. What we are trying to show is that families within the church are called to function as church in the home, since the impact of relationships within the family is so irrefutably formative, especially for children.

I hope it has become clear from our discussion that to function "as church" in the home does not mean taking on all the functions of a congregation. Rather it means living together in ways that express Christian faith and promote spiritual growth within the context of domestic life. The family is not a substitute for the congregation but a vital part of its larger structure. Therefore the family cannot afford to ignore the worship, teaching, and fellowship of the church any more than the church can afford to ignore the spiritually formative impact of the family. Each needs the other to fulfill its particular mission in a complementary manner.

If we can begin to see the family of faith as a specific expression of the church at large, I believe we will gain greater clarity about the most creative ways for the gathered church and the domestic church to relate to each other.

## The Relationship of Congregation and Family

Like Christian families, congregations are a specific expression of the church universal. They represent a family of faith whose parameters are broader than those of kinship families. As such, congregations reveal more fully the inclusiveness of God's kingdom and stand sentry against the danger of idolizing the nuclear family. In God's household, every kind of family structure is subjugated to a higher vision and its value radically reinterpreted. The criterion for membership in God's household, as we have seen, is obedience to the will of God. Our brothers and sisters in Christ may be complete strangers from the perspective of social convention, but they will not be strangers to us in spirit if they share a passion for the love of God.

Congregations often need to help member families move beyond the cultural idolatry and privatization of family life. It is part of the church's task to hold up authentic kingdom values and behaviors for its members to live out in the world. However, congregations are not immune to the seductive powers of the culture. As suggested earlier, sometimes the ministry of particular families within the church can help a congregation remain faithful to its call. Dolores Leckey maintains that the domestic church has much to teach the gathered church about what it means to live together creatively and faithfully.[4]

Nonetheless, families today often feel besieged by overwhelming demands, and they are greatly in need of support. With all the forms of ministry that are intrinsic and unique to family life—the daily nurture, care, and training that are means of God's grace within the home—it is a great challenge for church families simply to remain faithful to this calling. Pressure from jobs, schools, civil groups, relatives, and friends can be experienced as impediments to fulfilling the primary role of the family. One of the supports a congregation may be able to provide in such circumstances is helping families discern when these "impediments" are opportunities to express a wider calling to ministry in the community and when they are truly obstacles to the essential functions of family life.

By far the most vital service a congregation can provide for its families is genuine affirmation and support for the central and irreplaceable role that the domestic church plays in Christian spiritual formation. If the gathered church truly comprehends the central mission of family life within its body, I believe its approach to family ministry will be altered significantly. The church will be better able to acknowledge that, even when broken and incomplete, families are loved and blessed by God and graciously given gifts to fulfill their unique vocation. Families will be called, like the gathered church, to become places of redemptive transformation, not only for the sake of their own members but for the sake of the world.

The gathered church will need to lift up a vision of marriage and family as a place of holiness, beauty, and spiritual vitality and to support that vision through preaching, teaching, and programming. The church needs to supply what society no longer provides; namely, a view of marriage as a holy vocation. If Christian marriage is seen as a call to live together in a way that reveals God's faithful love, marriage becomes a witness to the wider world and not merely an end in itself.

The issue here goes beyond the question of *what* theology of marriage the church teaches to the question of *when* it is communicated. Many of us hear the church's teaching on marriage only in wedding services, a time of heightened emotion, frazzled nerves, and sentimentalized ideals of beauty and perfection. The church's theology of marriage should be a more central and regular feature of its teaching and preaching ministries, especially in a time when cultural stresses are so destructive of this basic building block of family life.

Yet the vision we are speaking of needs more than remote reinforcement through sermons, liturgy, and good teaching. It also needs personal, interactive reinforcement. If Christian marriage is a vocation, then preparation for it should be far more extensive and serious-minded than it is in most churches. How many of us would consider the choice of a life-partner to be a matter of spiritual discernment rather than of mere personal preference? Even if we agree that it should be a matter of careful discernment, how many of us would see that process as one involving the community of faith in some significant way? The Quakers have a tradition that involves a young couple in a process of discernment with the elders of the meeting before a decision for marriage is made. Here individual perceptions can be met and either affirmed or countered in love by the discernment of a community of faith.[5] This runs strongly against the grain of our cultural predilection for independent and autonomous individual choice. But a Christian marriage takes place in the context of a community of faith—both in discerning the call and in supporting that call through a lifetime.

Beyond vigorous marriage preparation, naturally congregations will want to provide enrichment and ongoing learning opportunities for couples growing across years of change. The fact that most marriages result in children raises another set of spiritual questions. Does it ever occur to us that *children are also a vocation?* Instead of assuming that children are a given, do we perceive that God *calls* us to be parents and even chooses to give us particular children? What would such an understanding imply for church families? Does it suggest that people need preparation for the vocation of child rearing, just as they need preparation for the vocation of marriage?

Our society evidently needs basic parenting skills. No consistent arena in our culture teaches us parenting skills apart from our own experience of being parented, which may or may not be a helpful model. Therefore it is appropriate for congregations to provide what they can, perhaps in cooperation with community social agencies and / or other congregations. Classes for parents at various stages of child rearing can prove enormously valuable, especially in the realm of what constitutes healthy communication, the positive and appropriate use of discipline, and changing roles through a child's development—the gradual but difficult process of allowing the child's autonomy to emerge. All of these and more may all be understood as ways in which the church prepares parents for the vocation of child rearing.

Yet what remains distinctive to the church is the spiritual dimension of life. It belongs to the church's ministry to help people discover the relationship between good parenting skills and spiritual nurture—their children's and their own. (I heard an adage recently to this effect: *The miracle is not that adults produce children, but that children produce adults!* )

The church also has something distinctive to offer in our culture when it comes to stressing the value not just of *quality time* but of *adequate time* with children. That is because faith offers a different perspective on the nature of time itself, its purpose and its use. What we accomplish, achieve, and acquire is understood to have value only within the larger compass of who we are in relation to one another and to God. The church may be in a position to encourage those families who are *able*—I am well aware that not all are able—to make financial and lifestyle sacrifices in order to provide adequate parental presence and nurture in their children's lives, especially in the early years. This has been a major issue for baby boomers, who are attracted to greater lifestyle comfort than their parents but who also want healthy families. The church is in a position to help new parents see how critical their choices are and what criteria make for wise choices.

In relation to child rearing, the church can also help parents accept the choices their growing children make that break some of the bonds parents nurture so intentionally. Will Willimon tells of a young woman in his congregation who got really excited about her faith and wanted to do a term of missionary service abroad. Her father, a well-placed physician, had expected her to continue her medical studies and follow the family tradition of doctoring. He was furious and came to Willimon to express his displeasure at the influence the church was exerting on his daughter. Will asked him, "Did you have her baptized?"

"Of course we had her baptized," the man replied.

"And did you bring her to Sunday school?"

"Sure we did."

"Well, then," said Willimon, "the damage was done long before now. You should have thought about what you were doing before you had her baptized!"[6] Obedience to God's call is a higher loyalty than to parental expectations.

To support the family in its spiritual vocation, churches will want to identify and make available good resources on child rearing, home worship, prayer, ritual, seasonal celebration, family retreats, service opportunities, and other practices fitting to family spiritual development. Reserve a section of the church library for such resources and strongly encourage families to make full use of it. But be aware that it will take active teaching and modeling to get most families creatively engaged with such resources. Suffering from ingrained habits of dependence on professionals, many adults simply do not know how to begin spiritual practices at home. They often lack confidence in their skills for communicating faith. Some fear resistance from family members and worry that their efforts may be perceived as hokey, controlling, or simply as a failure.

So churches need to develop "hands on" workshops and classes that enable parents to integrate their daily practical care of children with spiritual development. Adults need assistance with ways to pray and worship at home, as well as concrete helps with ritual and faith celebration. The best way to teach such practices is through events provided for the whole family instead of age-segregated groups. These should be fun and celebratory in character, although incorporating quiet reflection time is appropriate if the church wishes to model a contemplative dimension to worship in the home.

An important component of church education for families is the recovery of fresh, experiential language for faith. If one of the most fundamental gifts a parent can give a child is words to articulate inner experience, one of the greatest gifts a church can offer its families is faith language that is real, meaningful, and uncontrived. Older forms of religious language are often felt to be artificial, a block to the authenticity with which contemporary family members express their spiritual quest and experience to one another. Recovering clear, simple language is one way in which the gathered church can help the domestic church remove barriers inhibiting the fulfillment of its role in spiritual formation.

The congregation also provides a natural opportunity for families to *network* with other persons and families of faith. No single family unit can bear the burden of living faithfully out of its own resources alone. The notion of superfamilies who "have it all together" merely reinforces a destructive idealization and idolatry of the family. Families need to understand that accepting limits is not only permissible but essential. Learning when to say no is one of the great disciplines of our time. The support of other families or individuals with wisdom and experience can help the domestic church set priorities and make choices in the face of limited time, energy, and resources. Perhaps even more significantly, church families can join together in discerning one another's gifts and special calls to service. Too many congregations are notoriously unconscious of their own members' gifts and graces. One of the most life-affirming and energizing ways in which the gathered church can support its domestic members is to help them name and claim their God-given gifts. Church families can help one another discover the forms of ministry to which God is calling them.

Finally, the larger church always needs to be prepared to support families during times of crisis, loss, and confusion. This may call for creative intervention, pastoral counsel, or referral to other professionals. It may mean helping families to recognize and name the dynamics at work in their life together so that these can be confessed and opened to God's healing. In either case, the gathered church can help its domestic partners feel a sense of worth and take heart in the transforming grace of God.

Clearly I am promoting a theological understanding of the Christian family as a domestic expression of the church itself. The church is the instrument through which God calls families of faith to exercise their own ministry with children—a ministry so unique nothing can fully substitute for it; a ministry of reflecting and embodying God's love to one another in the home. The first task of the larger church with respect to its families is to give them a vision—a spiritual and theological vision—of who they are, what they are called to, and how their family life connects with the depths of their faith. The starting point is to help families of faith perceive themselves as embodiments of the church in their home life together.

## Conclusions

I have argued a particular thesis in this book: Families are, by virtue of their social function, primary arenas for personal and spiritual formation, whether that formation is destructive or life-giving. I have pointed out that families may choose to be intentional about the formative character of their life together and that families within the church are called to live out their Christian faith within the context of family life. Finally, I have stressed that if churches desire family formation to be explicitly Christian, they bear responsibility for helping families learn intentional Christian practices in the home, since the absence of such practices can scarcely be compensated for by the larger church. Indeed, the primary ministry of the gathered church to the domestic church is to remind the family of its graced task and to support it in its essential vocation. In this way, the church sets the family free for mission instead of using up family resources for institutional maintenance.

My hope is not to burden the family with more things to do in an already crowded and stressful life. It is, rather, to help the family of faith see and understand its spiritual vocation. It is to encourage families to take heart from the simple truth that the

Christian spiritual life can be lived within the very structures of ordinary family life and need not be sought in ascetic feats, lengthy retreats, or solely in the activities of the local congregation. Families of faith can make faithful choices about their use of time, they can be intentional about structuring spiritual practices in the home, and they can view the ordinary events of life together as windows onto God's abundant grace.

One of the most serious tasks of the church at large is to help its member families to *be* the body of Christ within the home—to become settings where unconditional love, affirmation, challenge to accountability, and forgiveness are known; to learn and share rituals, symbols, and stories of faith; to recognize and claim their special gifts and mission in the world. Then, as particular expressions of the all-inclusive family of God, church families become redeeming communities and thus sacraments of God's grace. Over two centuries ago Jonathan Edwards identified the importance of the family in faith development:

> Every Christian family ought to be as it were a little church consecrated to Christ, and wholly influenced and governed by his rule. And family education and order are some of the chief means of grace. If these fail, all other means are likely to prove ineffectual. If these are duly maintained, all the means of grace will be likely to prosper and be successful.[7]

May we find in these words both challenge and courage to join the joyful task of giving ourselves fully to God in the fabric of everyday life, there to be met by the grace that alone draws us to our final destiny in Christ.

## *For Reflection*

~ How would you describe the relationship between the church and the family of committed faith from a theological standpoint?

~ How do you experience the church's current support for its families?

~ In what ways could your congregation better support the vocation of families in faith?

# Notes

~

## Introduction

1. This is due to the tendency evident in recent national history to identify the Christian family uncritically with the myth of a "Christian America." See Robert T. Handy, *A Christian America: Protestant Hopes and Historical Realities* (New York: Oxford, 1971)

2. Parker J. Palmer, "The Spiritual Life: Apocalypse Now," in *Living with Apocalypse: Spiritual Resources for Social Compassion*, ed. Tilden H. Edwards (San Francisco: Harper & Row, 1984); 27, 29.

## Chapter 1

1. M. Robert Mulholland, Jr., *Shaped by the Word: The Power of Scripture in Spiritual Formation* (Nashville, TN: The Upper Room, 1985), 28.

2. Mulholland, *Shaped by the Word*, 27.

3. Dolores R. Leckey, *The Ordinary Way: A Family Spirituality* (New York: Crossroad, 1982), 52.

4. Rita Ann Houlihan, C.S.

5. Craig Dykstra makes a case for the idea that lifetime promises of commitment to one another constitute the essential characteristic of all family relationships, even, implicitly, the relationship of children with their parents, by virtue of response. See "Family Promises: Faith and Families in the Context of the Church," in *Faith and Families,* ed. Lindell Sawyers (Philadelphia: Geneva Press, 1986), 141.

6. Pope Paul VI, "Dogmatic Constitution on the Church," in *The Documents of Vatican II*, ed. Walter M. Abbot, S.J. (Baltimore: America Press, 1966), 29.

7. Edward Hays, *Prayers for the Domestic Church: A Handbook for Worship in the Home* (Leavenworth, KS: Forest of Peace Books, 1989), 17.

8. Hays, *Prayers for the Domestic Church*, 17.

9. John H. Westerhoff III, *Bringing Up Children in the Christian Faith* (Minneapolis, MN: Winston Press, 1980), 7.

10. Esther deWaal, "The Extraordinary in the Ordinary," *Weavings* 2 (May-June 1987): 15.

11. See *The Practice of the Presence of God*, a compilation of letters by, conversations with, and reminiscences about Brother Lawrence of the Resurrection. There is a new translation by Robert J. Edmonson, ed. Hal M. Helms (Orleans, MA: Paraclete Press, 1985).

12. See Evelyn Underhill, *Practical Mysticism* (New York: E.P. Dutton, 1943).

13. See Wendy M. Wright, "In the Circle of a Mother's Arms," *Weavings* 3 (Jan.-Feb. 1988): 14–23.

## Chapter 2

1. Deotis Roberts, *Roots of a Black Future: Family and Church* (Philadelphia: The Westminster Press, 1980), 33. For much of the perspective on black families expressed here, I am indebted to Dr. Roberts's elucidating work.

2. Quoted in Roberts, *Roots of a Black Future*, 33 (no reference given).

3. An insight gained from conversation with Professor Walter Fluker of Vanderbilt Divinity School, who cited Martin Luther King, Jr., and Howard Thurman as examples of black leaders whose faith was deeply formed by their grandmothers.

4. Cynthia M. Taeuber, *Sixty-Five Plus in America*, Current Population Reports, Special Studies, P23-178RV (Washington: U.S. Government Printing Office, 1991), 2.

5. *Information Please Almanac 1995* (Boston: Houghton Mifflin, 1995), 837.

6. Taeuber cites Elaine M. Brody, "Parent Care as a Normative Family Stress," *Gerontologist*, Feb. 1985, 19–29.

7. U.S. Bureau of the Census, *Statistical Abstract of the United States 1995* (Washington: U.S. Government Printing Office, 1995); 434, 63.

8. Steve W. Ramilings and Arlen F. Slauter, *Household and Family Characteristics: March 1994,* U.S. Bureau of the Census, Current Population Reports P20-483 (Washington: U.S. Government Printing Office, 1995), vii.

9. *Household and Family Characteristics*, vii.

10. *Universal Almanac 1995* (Kansas City: Andrews & McMeel, 1994), 307.

11. *The World Almanac and Book of Facts 1995* (Mahwah, NJ: World Almanac, 1994), 957.

12. *Statistical Abstract*, 479; *1990 Census of Population: Social and Economic Characteristics, U.S. 1990*, CP 2 1 (Washington: U.S. Government Printing Office, 1993), 2.

13. *Universal Almanac*, 305; *World Almanac*, 961.

14. *Universal Almanac*, 303.

15. *Statistical Abstract*, 479; *1990 Census of Population: Social and Economic Characteristics, U.S. 1990*, CP -2-1 (Washington: U.S. Government Printing Office, 1993), 2.

16. *World Almanac*, 960.

17. Dykstra, "Family Promises," 138.

18. Sheek, *The Word on Families*, 56.

19. "Habits of the Hearth," an interview conducted with Robert Bellah by Rodney Clapp, printed in *Christianity Today*, 33 (February 3, 1989): 22.

20. Clapp, "Habits of the Hearth," 22.

21. U.S. Bureau of the Census, *Household and Family Characteristics: March 1985* (Washington D.C.), P-20, No. 411.

22. See John Meyendorff, *Marriage: An Orthodox Perspective* (Crestwood, NY: St. Vladimir's Seminary Press, 1975) 60-65.

23. Leo Tolstoy, *Anna Karenina* (Garden City, NY: Garden City Publishing Co., 1948), 3.

24. Ron James, retired pastor of the First Presbyterian Church of Stamford, Connecticut, originally applied this memorable phrase to himself.

## Chapter 3

1. *Universal Almanac*, 303.
2. Harriet A. Washington, "Hospitals Test Medicine's Moral Responsibility," *Emerge*, June 1994, 22.
3. Gerald G. May, *Addiction and Grace* (San Francisco: Harper & Row, 1988), 3.
4. Robert N. Bellah et al., *Habits of the Heart: Individualism and Commitment in American Life* (Berkeley: University of California Press, 1985), 251.
5. Bellah, *Habits of the Heart*, 285.
6. Clapp, "Habits of the Hearth," 24.
7. Bellah et al., *Habits of the Heart*, 134.
8. *Habits of the Heart.*, 101.
9. *Habits of the Heart*, 98.
10. Parker J. Palmer, *To Know as We Are Known* (San Francisco: Harper & Row, 1983), 37.
11. Many of these are plant and insect species not yet catalogued by scientists, according to the private environmental group The Nature Conservancy.

## Chapter 4

1. Dolores Leckey's title phrase; see "Sacred Shelters," *Living with Apocalypse*, ed. Tilden H. Edwards, 171.
2. Leckey, "Sacred Shelters,", 172.
3. Leckey, "Sacred Shelters,", 172.
4. Wendy Wright, "Finding God in Family Life," *Praying* magazine, Nov.–Dec. 1987; 6, 8.
5. Wright, "Finding God in Family Life," 6–7.
6. See Ralph Mattson and Thom Black, *Discovering Your Child's Design* (Elgin, IL: David C. Publishing Co., 1992), 189–97.
7. For this insight I am indebted to Anthony Bloom, *Living Prayer* (Springfield, IL: Templegate Publishers, 1966), 31.
8. Lewis Smedes, *Forgive and Forget: Healing the Hurts We Don't Deserve* (San Francisco: HarperSanFrancisco, 1984), xii.

9. Jesse Kornbluth, "The Woman Who Beat the Klan," *New York Times Magazine*, November 1, 1987, 38.

10. Ernest Boyer, Jr., *A Way in the World: Family Life as Spiritual Discipline* (San Francisco: Harper & Row, 1984), 66.

11. Leckey, *The Ordinary Way*, 133.

12. Elizabeth Yates, *A Book of* (Nashville, TN: Upper Room Books, 1989), 27.

13. See Carol Dittberner, "The Pure Wonder of Young Lives," *Sojourners* 16 (January 1987): 21.

14. Sofia Cavalletti, *The Religious Potential of the Child* (New York: Paulist Press, 1982); 44, 45.

15. Cavalletti, *The Religious Potential of the Child*, 31–32.

16. *Padre Dimitri Dudko*, "Parroco a Mosca. Conversazioni serali," Quaderni della *Rivista del Centro studi Russia cristiana* (Milano: 1976), pp. 144–45.

17. Dittberner, "The Pure Wonder of Young Lives," 24.

## Chapter 5

1. Cited in Kenneth Leech, *True Prayer: An Invitation to Christian Spirituality* (San Francisco: Harper & Row, 1980), 9.

2. John Calvin, *Institutes of the Christian Religion*, ed. John T. McNeill, trans. F. L. Battles (Philadelphia: The Westminster Press, 1977), 850–51.

3. E. M. Bounds, *Power through Prayer* (Chicago: Moody Press, n.d.), 38; cited in Richard J. Foster, *The Celebration of Discipline: Paths to Spiritual Growth* (San Francisco: HarperSanFrancisco, 1988), 34.

4. Bounds, *Power through Prayer*, 23; cited in Foster, *The Celebration of Discipline*, 34.

5. Foster, *The Celebration of Discipline*, 44.

6. Foster, *The Celebration of Discipline*, 41–42.

7. T. S. Eliot, "Ash Wednesday" in *The Complete Poems and Plays 1909–1950* (New York: Harcourt Brace Jovanovich, 1971), 67.

8. See DelBene, *The Breath of Life: A Simple Way to Pray* (Minneapolis, MN: Winston Press, 1981). For much of what

follows in this section, I am indebted to Ron's teachings and writings on this topic.

9. Ron DelBene, *Into the Light: A Simple Way to Pray for the Sick and the Dying*, written with Mary and Herb Montgomery (Nashville, TN: The Upper Room, 1988).

10. Thomas R. Kelly, *A Testament of Devotion* (New York: Harper & Brothers, 1941), 35.

11. *The Practice of the Presence of God*; 79, 93.

12. The Reverend Bruce Ough, currently serving as district superintendent of the Cedar Rapids district, Iowa Annual Conference, The United Methodist Church.

13. Author Henri Nouwen made a similar point in "Spirituality and the Family," *Weavings* 3 (Jan.-Feb. 1989): 9. For insights related to the necessity of solitude in all forms of community, I am indebted to Henri's writings and teachings over the course of many years.

## Chapter 6

1. Gertrud Mueller Nelson, *To Dance with God: Family Ritual and Community Celebration* (New York: Paulist Press, 1986), 150. Her book is a virtual gold mine of family rituals and community celebrations, 41.

2. See Dittberner, "The Pure Wonder of Young Lives," 22.

3. *Daily Prayer: The Worship of God*, Supplemental Liturgical Resource 5, prepared by the Office of Worship for the Presbyterian Church (U.S.A.) and the Cumberland Presbyterian Church (Philadelphia: Westminster Press, 1987), 16.

4. *Book of Common Worship: Daily Prayer*, prepared by the Theology and Worship Unit for the Presbyterian Church (U.S.A.) and the Cumberland Presbyterian Church (Louisville, KY: Westminster / John Knox Press, 1993).

5. Mueller Nelson, *To Dance with God*, 25–26.

6. Mueller Nelson, *To Dance with God*, 83.

7. Mueller Nelson, *To Dance with God*, 143–44.

8. I have treated this distinction more fully in my book *Soul Feast: An Invitation to the Christian Spiritual Life* (Louisville, KY: Westminster / John Knox Press, 1995), chapter 6.

9. Thompson, *Soul Feast*, chapter 5.
10. Mueller Nelson, *To Dance with God*, 150
11. Mueller Nelson, *To Dance with God*, 223–30.

## Chapter 7

1. Mulholland, *Shaped by the Word*; 34, 36.
2. For the image of the iconographic nature of scripture, I am again indebted to the writing of Robert Mulholland.
3. *The Children's Bible* (New York: Golden Press, 1965).
4. Phrase used by Thomas R. Hawkins in *The Unsuspected Power of the Psalms* (Nashville, TN: The Upper Room, 1985), 16.
5. Leckey, *The Ordinary Way*, 67.
6. See Boyer, *A Way in the World*, chapter 4 and page 57.
7. For a more extensive description of the spiritual guide as midwife, see Tilden H. Edwards, *Spiritual Friend: Re claiming the Gift of Spiritual Direction* (New York: Paulist Press, 1980).
8. Please note that this process is *not* appropriate for severe interpersonal problems within the family. In cases of alcohol or drug abuse, child or spouse abuse, spouse hostility leading toward separation or divorce, teenage pregnancy or other serious teen problems, the family needs professional counsel. A dysfunctional family will need substantial social and psychological help in addition to spiritual help.
9. Walter Brueggemann, "The Commandments and Liberated, Liberating Bonding," *Journal for Preachers* 10, no. 2 (1987): 19.

## Chapter 8

1. Douglas V. Steere, *Dimensions of Prayer* (New York: Women's Division, Board of Global Ministries, The United Methodist Church, 1962), 80.
2. Gwen White leads conferences, retreats, and seminars on the spirituality of the family. I have drawn on material she presented for the Consultation on Family Spirituality sponsored by The Upper Room in Nashville, Tennessee, in April 1986.
3. Leckey, *The Ordinary Way*, 143–44.

4. James McGinnis and Kathleen McGinnis, "The Social Mission of the Family," in *Faith and Families*, 90–91.
5. McGinnis, "The Social Mission of the Family," 105.
6. Drawn from materials presented at the Consultation on Family Spirituality sponsored by The Upper Room in Nashville, Tennessee, in April 1986.
7. "Educational Ministry of the Presbyterian Church (U.S.A.)" A Paper for Reflection and Discussion [Church Education Services, Program Agency, Presbyterian Church (U.S.A.), 1984], 19, cited in McGinnis and McGinnis, "The Social Mission of the Family," 100.
8. "Lineamenta: The Role of the Christian Family in the Modern World" (Washington, D.C.: U.S. Catholic Conference, 1979), 44; cited in McGinnis and McGinnis "Social Mission of the Family," 100.
9. *The Evelyn Underhill Reader*, comp. Thomas S. Kepler (Nashville, TN: Abingdon Press, 1962), 95.
10. A paraphrase of Bishop J. Francis Stafford by Leckey, *The Ordinary Way*, 143.

## Chapter 9

1. Paraphrased from Boyer, *A Way in the World*, 35–36.
2. Sang H. Lee, "The Importance of the Family: A Reformed Theological Perspective," in *Faith and Families*, 115–35.
3. Parker J. Palmer, *The Company of Strangers: Christians and the Renewal of America's Public Life* (New York: Crossroad, 1983), 124.
4. From the Consultation on Family Spirituality sponsored by The Upper Room, April 1986.
5. For a helpful description of such a practice, see Richard Foster's *The Celebration of Discipline*, chap. 12, especially pages 181–82.
6. Verified and used by permission of William H. Willimon.
7. Clyde A. Holbrook, *The Ethics of Jonathan Edwards: Morality and Aesthetics* (Ann Arbor: University of Michigan Press, 1973), 83.

# Bibliography

—— ∽ ——

## Books available for purchase

Achtemeier, Elizabeth. *The Committed Marriage*. Philadelphia, PA: Westminster / John Knox Press, 1976.

Boyer, Ernest, *Finding God at Home: Family Life as Spiritual Discipline*. San Francisco: HarperSanFrancisco, 1988.

Broyles, Anne. *Growing Together in Love: God Known through Family Life*. Nashville, TN: Upper Room Books, 1993.

Cavalletti, Sofia. *The Religious Potential of the Child: Experiencing Scripture and Liturgy with Young Children*. Chicago: Liturgy Training Publications, 1992.

Cecil, Nancy Lee. *Raising Peaceful Children in a Violent World*. San Diego, CA: LuraMedia, 1995.

Coles, Robert. *The Spiritual Life of Children*. Boston: Houghton Mifflin Company, 1991.

DelBene, Ron. *The Breath of Life: A Simple Way to Pray*. Nashville, TN: Upper Room Books, 1992.

_____. *Into the Light: A Simple Way to Pray with the Sick and the Dying*. Nashville, TN: Upper Room Books, 1988.

DeVries, Mark. *Family-Based Youth Ministry: Reaching the Been-There, Done-That Generation*. Downers Grove, IL: InterVarsity Press, 1994.

Eastman, Moira. *Family: The Vital Factor*. San Francisco: HarperSanFrancisco, 1991.

Evans, James L. *Bringing God Home: Family Devotions for the Christian Year*. Macon, GA: Smyth and Helwys Publishing, Inc., 1995.

Foster, Richard J. *Celebration of Discipline: The Path to Spiritual Growth*. San Francisco: HarperSanFrancisco, 1988.

Fuchs, Nancy. *Our Share of Night, Our Share of Morning: Parenting as a Spiritual Journey*. San Francisco: HarperSanFrancisco, 1996.

Garborg, Rolf. *The Family Blessing: A Simple Parental Act That Will Help Your Children Feel Loved and Cherished*. Dallas, TX: Word Publishing, 1994.

Halverson, Delia. *How Do Our Children Grow?* Nashville, TN: Abingdon Press, 1993.

Hays, Edward. *Prayers for the Domestic Church: A Handbook for Worship in the Home*. Leavenworth, KS: Forest of Peace Publishing, Inc., 1989.

Heller, David. *The Children's God*. Chicago: The University of Chicago Press, 1986.

_____. *Talking to Your Child about God: A Book for Families of All Faiths*. New York: Berkley Publishing, 1994.

Herbert, Christopher. *Prayers for Children*. Cincinnati, OH: Forward Movement Publications, 1994.

Linthorst, Ann T. *Mothering as a Spiritual Journey: Learning to Let God Nurture Your Children and You Along with Them*. New York: Crossroad, 1993.

Luebering, Carol. *The Forgiving Family: First Steps to Reconciliation*. Cincinnati, OH: Saint Anthony Messenger Press, 1983.

Mattson, Ralph, and Thom Black. *Discovering Your Child's Design*. Elgin, IL: David C. Cook Publishing Co., 1989.

Nelsen, Jane. *Positive Discipline*. New York: Ballantine Books, Inc., 1996.

Nelson, Gertrud Mueller. *To Dance with God: Family Ritual and Community Celebration*. Mahwah, NJ: Paulist Press, 1986.

Pipher, Mary. *The Shelter of Each Other: Rebuilding Our Families*. Ballantine Books, Inc., 1997.

Shedd, Charlie W. *Letters to Karen: On Keeping Love in Marriage*. New York: Avon Books, 1976.

Smedes, Lewis B. *Forgive and Forget: Healing the Hurts We Don't Deserve*. San Francisco: HarperSanFrancisco, 1984.

Smylie, Betsy D. and John S. *Christian Parenting*. Nashville, TN: Upper Room Books, 1991.

Weaver, Judy. *Celebrating Holidays and Holy Days in Church and Family Settings*. Nashville, TN: Discipleship Resources, 1989.

Westerhoff, John H. III. *Will Our Children Have Faith?* San Francisco: HarperSanFrancisco, 1983.

Wright, Wendy M. *Sacred Dwelling: A Spirituality of Family Life*. Leavenworth, KS: Forest of Peace Publishing, Inc., 1994.

Wuellner, Flora Slosson. *Release: Healing from Wounds of Family, Church, and Community*. Nashville, TN: Upper Room Books, 1996.

## Books available in libraries or church resource centers

Held, Ann Reed. *Keeping Faith in Families*. Belleville, IL: National Presbyterian Mariners, 1987.

Leckey, Dolores R. *The Ordinary Way: A Family Spirituality*. NY: Crossroad, 1982.

Sawyers, Lindell, ed. *Faith and Families*. Philadelphia: Geneva Press, 1986.

Sheek, G. William. *The Word on Families: A Biblical Guide to Family Well-Being*. Nashville, TN: Abingdon Press, 1985.

Westerhoff, John H. III. *Bringing Up Children in the Christian Faith*. Minneapolis, MI: Winston Press, 1980.

## Periodicals

*Devo'Zine*. A devotional magazine for teens. Published bi-monthly by The Upper Room. Daily meditations, feature articles, prayers, scripture, reflection questions, topical index. Lively four-color format.

*Pockets*. A devotional magazine specially designed for *children*. Published monthly (except Jan / Feb) by The Upper Room. Excellent stories, poems, prayers and meditations, service suggestions, and a calendar of scripture readings.

*Weavings* 3, no. 1 (January-February 1988). "Family Life" issue.

*Weavings* 7, no. 2 (March-April 1992). "Forgiveness" issue.

**To order periodicals listed above, call 1-800-925-6847.**

## Other Print Resources

*Jan's Learning Tree*. A catalog of music, toys, games, books, videos to promote positive self-esteem, imagination, creativity, and cooperation with children. Excellent and thoughtful collection of resources. Write 3205 New Towne Road, Antioch, TN 37013-1220.

*To Celebrate: Reshaping Holidays and Rites of Passage*. An Alternatives publication. Write Alternatives, P. O. Box 429, Ellenwood, GA 30049.

*Whose Birthday Is It, Anyway?* An Alternatives publication (see address above). Other seasonal resources available also.

*Families Matter: A Planning Resource*. Order from Office of Family Ministries and Conference Relations, The

General Board of Discipleship, The United Methodist Church, P. O. Box 840, Nashville, TN 37202.

*Homeward Bound: Families Moving into the 21st Century.* Congregational study guide. Write United Church of Canada, Family Ministries, 85 St. Clair Ave. East, Toronto, Ontario, M4T 1MB.

## Videos

*The Family Matters.* A series of six videos on the following topics: Working Parents, Parents of Teenagers, People with Aging Parents, Single Parents, Blended Families, Parents Living Apart from Their Children. Order from EcuFilm, 810 12th Ave. South, Nashville, TN 37203 or call 1-800-251-4091.

*Active Parenting.* A six-part series on parenting skills. Write Active Parenting, 810 Franklin Court, Suite B, Marietta, GA 30067 or call 1-800-825-0060.

*Parenting for Life.* A twelve-part series in Christian parenting, set within in biblical and theological frameowrk. Write Parenting for Life, 2234 Hyalea Road, Tucker, GA 30084.

*Spirited Families.* Helps families reflect on their values and the relationship of faith to family living. Write United Church of Canada, Family Ministries, 85 St. Clair Ave., East, Toronto, Ontario M4T 1MB.

*Stones of Promise.* A thirteen-part video with study guide. Deals with African American families, traditions, conflicts, and faith journeys. Write American Baptist Churches Educational Ministries, P. O. Box 851, Valley Forge, PA 19482-0851

## Organizations

National Center for Fathering: 217 Southwind Place, Manhattan, KS 66502. A center committed to strengthening the constructive role fathers play in the lives of their children.

Focuses on providing positive father models, encouraging healthy relational patterns in the home, and valuing the unique intergenerational roles of men in family life.

National Presbyterian Mariners: 3704 North Belt West, Belleville, IL 62223. Has programs and resources available for single parents, couples with or without children, and intergenerational families. Offers marriage enrichment resources, mission opportunities, conferences, and meaningful vacation options for families.

Family Service America: 11700 West Lake Park Drive, Park Place; Milwaukee, WS 53224. Discusses strengthening family life through problem solving: assistance with marital difficulties, parent-child tension, drug and alcohol dependency, teenage pregnancy, aging-parent care, child abuse, family violence, and other problems.

RELATED BOOKS OF INTEREST
FROM UPPER ROOM BOOKS

*Children and Prayer: A Shared Pilgrimage,* by
Betty Shannon Cloyd
ISBN 0-8358-0803-3

*Growing Compassionate Kids: Helping Kids See
Beyond their Backyard,* by Jan Johnson
ISBN 0-8358-0932-3

*Parents and Grandparents as Spiritual Guides:
Nurturing Children of the Promise,* by Betty
Shannon Cloyd
ISBN 0-8358-0923-4

Order online at www.upperroom.org/bookstore

Order toll-free by phone 1-800-972-0433

Or find at your local bookstore